Pagan Portals

Grimalkyn:
The Witch's Cat

Power Animals in
Traditional Witchcraft

Pagan Portals

Grimalkyn:
The Witch's Cat

Power Animals in
Traditional Witchcraft

Martha Gray

Winchester, UK
Washington, USA

First published by Moon Books, 2013
Moon Books is an imprint of John Hunt Publishing Ltd., Laurel House, Station Approach,
Alresford, Hants, SO24 9JH, UK
office1@jhpbooks.net
www.johnhuntpublishing.com
www.moon-books.net

For distributor details and how to order please visit the 'Ordering' section on our website.

Text copyright: Martha Gray 2012

ISBN: 978 1 78099 956 2

A CIP catalogue record for this book is available from the British Library.

Design: Stuart Davies

Printed and bound by CPI Group (UK) Ltd, Croydon, CR0 4YY

We operate a distinctive and ethical publishing philosophy in all
areas of our business, from our global network of authors to
production and worldwide distribution.

CONTENTS

Introduction

There is no middle ground with cats – we either love them or loath them – but the cat adopted as a power animal represents independence, cunning, dexterity, agility, sensuality, inscrutability and ferocity. And whether the great wild hunter of forests, deserts or grasslands, or an ordinary domestic tabby, they *are* beautiful creatures. Some would dismiss them as merely killing machines, but we only have to look at the history of their evolution alongside mankind to realise there is nothing on this planet quite like them.

Cats have been on the receiving end of some cruel and barbaric treatment in the name of religion and superstition. But there have also been religions that honoured and deified them, with the lion and jaguar representing individual deities within ancient cultures; while representations of these sacred animals can still be seen today in the temples and tombs of the Egyptian kings.

In magical terms the cat has long been linked with traditional British witchcraft - in fact and fiction - and *Grimalkyn - The Witch's Cat* will reveal how this unique cat-power can be utilised in Circle workings. We need to be able to identify these unique energies, and the only way to reach this understanding is to take a peek into their world and see how they have evolved.

In some sections it may seem that some of the symbols and representations are duplicated. This is deliberate, as no matter which culture has recognised the feline magical energies in the past, they evolved to mean the same thing (or at least very similar) in symbolism and magical correspondences, even though these civilisations were thousands of miles (and even thousands of years) apart. Here we are identifying with the archetypes of Carl Jung's collective unconscious.

The magical exercises within this book are tried and tested working methods, together with instructions on how to perform them competently and safely. Hopefully, after reading *Grimalkyn - The Witch's Cat*, you will come to realise that these are more than just domestic pets, or a threatened wild species. Cats have helped shape religious belief and individual attitudes, while still maintaining an independent, and a sometimes, secretive nature.

Martha Gray

Derbyshire – 2012

PART ONE:

The Nature of the Beast

The naming of cats is a difficult matter.
It isn't just one of your holiday games.
You may think at first I'm as mad as a hatter.
When I tell you a cat has three different names.
'The Naming of Cats', *Old Possums Book of Practical Cats*
T S Eliot

Within magic, religion, mysticism and folklore, animals play a key role for humans on physical, psychological and spiritual levels. Cats, whether of the domestic variety, or one of the five 'Big Cats', are no exception. There is evidence of this recorded on ancient monuments, and in art and sculpture that has come down through the centuries: the finest example being those of ancient Egypt where monuments like the great Sphinx can still be marvelled at. The relationship between cat and human *is* a close one despite the historical love-hate reaction that has gone on for centuries, and the witch and magical practitioner with a feline power-animal is following a very ancient Path indeed.

Felines originally evolved between 65-33 million years ago from a species known as *miacids* - long-toothed, tree-climbing, carnivorous mammals. These creatures were intelligent hunters with the sharp teeth and claws to enable them to catch and eat their prey. This species split into two groups, and we can trace the ancestors of modern cats back about 11 million years with the emergence of the sub-species: *panthera* (roaring cat), *acinonyx* (cheetah) and *felis* (all other small cats).

According to Carl Jung, all living things belong to a collective unconscious - a set of primal instincts and behaviours within all life forms that have a nervous system. It is part of a genetic process that has been carried down through the ages, and passed on through DNA. These primal impulses can be tapped into when needed, or surface through instinct and intuition. Some call this the 'Akashic Records', an eastern term for 'ether' or 'the all', representing the multi-dimensional universe, or the universal brain.

This is not the same as our own *personal* unconscious that has been developed through our own personal experiences, those of our parents, social structure, upbringing; or information from our conscious mind that has been suppressed. This personal unconscious forms who we are as individuals and we need to make sure we know the difference between the two. With the theory in mind that we all come from the same source, it suggests that the most basic instinctive reactions that are present in *our* behaviour, are also present in other living organisms – like the cat family.

For magical purposes when attempting to harness cat-power we have to remember that although the animals appear similar, there are subtle differences, depending on which type of cat we choose to work with. This is due to their biology, environment and interaction with other species. For example:

Lions *(panthera leo)*

The second largest of the four big cats - tiger, leopard and jaguar - the only four that can roar and which are thought to have evolved into their class around 1.6 million years ago. They are muscular and stocky, which they use to their advantage in bringing down prey. Lions live in family groups, known as a 'pride' and are the only members of the cat family to do so, as the others are generally solitary. The males' main function, with a thick mane to protect them when fighting, is to protect the pride from outsiders including other lions, while the females do all the hunting and rearing the cubs. Symbolically, the lion represents kingship, strength, courage, honour and valour.

There are depictions of lions all over Europe, Asia, and the Middle East, with the most famous being those of ancient Egypt. The oldest images are the paintings in the Chauvet caves in France showing a lioness hunting, which are thought to be around 30,000 years old; and paintings of two lions mating in the 'Chamber of Felines' in the Lascaux caves. While a prehistoric ivory carving of a lion has been found in the Vogelherd cave in Germany.

Ancient cultures used lions to decorate great buildings in order to add majesty to the design, and were widespread throughout Mesopotamia. The gates of Mycenae in Greece also show two lioness-deities flanking a column; while in Turkey, the old Hittite city of Bogazkay, they adorn the walls of the gateways. Persia also used the image of lions on their gates to project the great majesty of their cities.

The Greeks saw lions as having not just the power of strength but also of invincibility. In the myth of the Twelve Labours of Hercules, his first task was to slay the Nemean Lion. The beast's golden fur was said to be impenetrable by any weapon, while its claws were sharper than any sword. Hercules eventually followed it into its lair and used his club to stun the lion, and then strangled it to death. He tried to remove the skin from the lion by using his knife but this did not work; the goddess Athena told him to use one of the lion's claws and he was able to take the fur to use as a cloak of invincibility. The Greeks identified the constellation of Leo with the Nemean lion.

Lions were not native to Southern Asia but their symbolism was believed to have been introduced by Buddhist monks in the first century AD, since they were considered to bring good luck and keep away evil spirits. In the Forbidden City in Beijing, there are two lions in every doorway, and during the Chinese New Year the lion dance is performed to scare away any evil spirits and to bring good luck in the coming year. Pairs of lion statues are found in other Southern Asian countries as guardians of gateways, along with statues of the winged lions found in doorways to temples in Indonesia. In Burma, the coat of arms is the *chinthe*, a lion or lion with a human face. The currency of Burma, the *kyat* also depicts a lion.

In Singapore the national flag has a creature on it called the *merlion* that has the head of a lion and the body of a fish. The name obviously deriving from *mer* = sea and lion. The body of the fish comes from Singapore's old ancient name of Temasek, which means 'sea town' and Singapura is the old original name which means 'lion city'. In Sri Lanka, the ethnic majority, are the Sinhalese people, whose name is derived from Ayan Sinhala which means the 'lion people' or 'people with lion blood'. Their flag still has the emblem of a lion with a sword.

In Hinduism the lion can be seen as one of the avatars of Vishnu, Narasima, who had the head and claws of a lion and the body of a human and was widely worshipped in temples across southern India as protector of his devoted worshippers. He was said to roam the mountain regions and when angered he was a dreaded wild beast, bringing terror to those who would harm his subjects. Lions were considered sacred to the Indian people and the motif of a lion on their flags and coat of arms has nothing to do with the British colonisation of the country. The name Singh is an ancient Vedic name for lion that can trace its origins back 2000 years, and is said to have originated with Rajputs, a Kshatriya or military caste.

Magical attributes

Here we see countries that have no indigenous connection with the lion, but who have adopted it as a symbol of strength and power. The lion is also the symbol of king and leadership, and must have had a very powerful effect on the human psyche. The lion's attributes are strength and courage, which can be harsh and tyrannical if not tempered with kindness. Its ruling planet is the Sun, the heavenly body at the centre of our solar system around which everything revolves. Although the Sun gives life and growth, it can also be destructive. This energy is also androgynous as both sexes are equally as powerful in their own right. The carnal aspects release a potent sexual energy that can be used magically to give a working 'super kick' and a strong sense of self-discipline is needed to direct these energies correctly. These power animals can be harnessed for protection as the lion would do for his pride and the lioness for her cubs. This energy is fierce and the magical practitioner should bear this in mind when working with leonine energy.

Tiger *(panthera tigris)*

The biggest of the 'Big Cats' which could once be found from Siberia to the mountain regions of Iran and Iraq. The markings on each tiger are individual just like that of the human fingerprint, with the red-brown colouring on the background of the stripes varying with the habitat. These are solitary creatures that need a vast amount of space for their territory and the only time that tigers come together is to mate. They are on the top ten list of endangered species with destruction of habitat and poaching (for skins and body parts to be used in Chinese medicine) as the main cause of the decline in their population.

It is ironic that the tiger is being hunted to extinction by Chinese poachers, because it was and still is one of the most sacred symbols of the Chinese people. It is a symbol of the male Yang principle and a solar symbol that gives a link to the season of summer. To the southern Chinese it was a symbol of war and the honorary symbol of the highest generals of the land as it represented courage, strength and power. There were five tigers that were honoured by the Chinese:

- The white tiger was a symbol of autumn and the element of Metal.
- The black tiger was that of winter and the element of

Water.

- The blue tiger was of spring and the element of Earth.
- The red tiger was the summer and the element of Fire.
- The yellow tiger was the governor of all the tigers and elements, and was the symbol of the Sun.

In Chinese martial arts, as well as other creatures like the crane, the movements that are enacted include those of the tiger. In Buddhism it represented one of the 'senseless creatures' - being that of the emotion of anger, and something that has to be tamed and controlled; in India, the goddess Durga, an aspect of the Great Mother who was a ten-armed war-goddess riding on the back of the tiger. Her name means 'invincible' and she was named as one of the forms of the wife of Shiva; she is a warrior who will go into battle to protect the gods in their time of need. The Siberian tiger was near deified by some of the tribal people of Russia: the Tungustic people called it 'Grandfather' or the 'Old Man'; while the Udege and the Nanai called it 'Amba'. The Maunu called it 'Hu Lin' - the king.

Magical attributes

Whatever the tradition, the tiger is the Eastern king of the beasts but do beware, as this big cat can be a friend or a foe to us depending on its mood. The tiger as a power animal is the Eastern equivalent of the lion, and should be viewed in this context when working with this cat-power on a magical level. The Element is Fire and represents strength, courage, bravery, protection and also a symbol of royalty and leadership. Like the lion the energy is fierce, but unlike the lion (whose is sociable and can be seen as a stable community protector), the tiger is solitary with the power of brute force. It also symbolises freedom and independence as these cats need huge territories to roam. Beware of the tiger's camouflaging stripes. This illusion can be used for glamour or protection; a warning to be wary. Those stripes also conceal a deadly force behind a calm watchful exterior and it takes a brave individual to look deep behind the stripes and embrace the raw force of the tiger.

Leopard *(panthera pardus)*

The smallest of the four members of the *panthera* family but no less formidable. It is now a near-threatened species due to loss of habitat and hunting, and is only found in South Africa, sub-Saharan Africa, Pakistan, India, Sri Lanka, Malaysia and China, although at one time it was well distributed over Africa, Asia and Siberia.

The leopard has a wide habitat that can range from rain forest to desert. It will catch and consume any animal it is able to hunt and has the widest 'prey menu' of any of the Big Cats. It is a nocturnal creature preferring to hunt between sunrise and sunset, being solitary and elusive animals they prefer to remain hidden from view until nightfall. It can climb trees better than any other feline and will drag a carcass up there to protect its food from other predators. They are agile with very strong leg muscles but prefer to hunt by stealth.

Magical attributes

The magical energy for the leopard is that of the carnal aspects that we will discuss in another chapter. It is also associated with fraud and hidden danger, while reminding us that nothing can change its innate nature. Anyone wishing to use the leopard as a power animal must realise that although it can help the witch or shaman to acquire hidden knowledge, it can also deliver false-hoods - something to bear in mind when journeying with *this* cat. Like the other felines their energy is solar-power, and in a magical working the leopard is swift and agile - its bite is powerful and severe

NB: With magical working there is a danger to confuse the normal leopard with the snow leopard. The characteristics of

the latter are different as they are more trusting of human beings - which is why they are easily hunted. Another factor to consider.

Black Panther

In the form of the 'black panther', the leopard's symbol becomes that of a darker, feminine aspect: that of the Dark Mother. Her realms are those of darkness, death and rebirth. The lunar significance is that of the Dark Moon. The black panther will help us overcome the fears of the psyche - of the unknown, darkness and death. It will teach us to harness the dark energy and gain a better understanding of it, since the human race has an inherent fear and prejudice of the unknown. It is not just physical death that this panther represents, but the death of certain ways of thinking, psychological blocks, and a way of life that no longer suits us because it causes pain, suffering and upheaval. Taking this journey can lead to major changes and a fresher outlook or perspective.

Magical attributes

The force of the panther is also believed to represent hidden pleasures within us all. This is a force that was recognised and respected by many ancient traditions all over the world. The power-panther, as opposed to that of the cat (which is similar but much stronger, more potent), can take us into the darkest regions of the psyche. The black panther as a power animal is ruled by lunar energy and represents discovery and mastery over our darkest nature. It reveals how burying our primal natures can cause unhealthy, unsettling thoughts and behaviour patterns - triggers for self-destruction and harm to those around us. Panther-power also represents birth, death and rebirth from the darker aspects of the feminine nature associated with deities such as Kali, Hecate, Tiamat and others of this strong primal vibration. For the shaman the leopard/panther skin was worn to represent the discovery of knowledge and wisdom.

We can also work with the panther to rid ourselves of our fear of the unknown, because understanding the thing you fear means it no longer has power over you.

Jaguar *(panthera onca)*

Another of the 'Big Cat' species and the only one of this group indigenous to South and Central America; it is the largest of the cats in the region and the third largest in the world. This cat's appearance is similar to that of the leopard; the noticeable difference being the size and build as it is much stockier. It mostly lives in the rainforests but is found in other forested areas and open country, especially near water. It is a solitary cat and a 'stalk and ambush' predator. Its jaws and teeth are exceptionally powerful and of all the cats it has the strongest bite. Its colour ranges from tawny to reddish to black with the spots very clearly defined on the face and tail. The rosettes on the body vary but the belly, throat and inner legs are white. Besides the size, the other differences between the leopard and the jaguar is that there are more spots on a leopard, and the rosettes on the jaguar are larger with spots in the centre - the spots usually darker than those of the leopard.

Magical attributes

The magical symbolism is that of strength in overcoming trials and initiatory principals. The mother-goddess of the South American tribes was represented by the jaguar; and it is a creature favoured by the shaman of this region. To the Aztecs, Tzcallipoca was a god who had many facets: representing the northern direction with the night winds, hurricanes, war, temptation and strife, and the night sky. His name means 'smoking mirror' and his associations are black obsidian (in the form of a mirror or ball) and the jaguar.

The jaguar's energies can be quite complex as they are dual

purpose. For those who follow the shamanic path, or those who wish to connect with stellar energies, the jaguar is the power animal to work with. By day they are the life-giving strength of the Sun while by night they are creatures that stalk the darkness and of the hidden realms - while also taking you to hidden depths of Self. The shaman used the skin of the jaguar to gain the power and strength of the animal while in a trance state and journeying through the other realms. The jaguar also has many facets and gaining wisdom from this cat will take a lifetime in itself.

Cheetah *(acinonyx jubatus)*

The cheetah is a species in its own right, evolving and separating from the other felines about 5.5 million years ago, inhabiting most of Africa and parts of the Middle East. Its notable feature is being the fastest mammal on the planet, and in short bursts can reach between 70 and 75 miles per hour with an acceleration of 0 to 62 miles per hour in 3 seconds! In short bursts they can cover 500 metres but this can only be kept up for a short time as the cheetah is not capable of running for long distances.

With a deep chest and narrow waist, the male is heavier than the female and with a slightly bigger head; it can sometimes be confused with the smaller variety of leopard, but the body of a leopard is longer while the cheetah has a longer tail. The coat is tan with white under parts, and round black spots that travel down the tail to merge into dark rings near the end and a white tuft. The tail is also used for steering while running and helps the animal to make sharp turns while trying to outwit its quarry. The familiar dark 'tear stains' distinguish them from the other spotted cats, running from the corner of the eyes down to the mouth - which apparently helps them to see long distance while hunting and to keep the sunlight from reflecting in their eyes. Cheetahs can purr but they cannot roar; they growl, chirrup, and make other chattering noises.

Cheetahs are less aggressive than other species so they can be tamed and were used like greyhounds to hunt antelope by the Egyptians, and later the Persians and Indians. As a result, they gained the status of the symbol of royalty. Akbar the Great of Mugbal was said to have had 1000 cheetahs as pets, and other leaders such as Genghis Khan was also said to keep them as pets, as well as for hunting. Even as late as the early 1930s the King of Ethiopia – the Lion of Judea - was pictured with cheetahs on a lead.

Magical attributes

The cheetah is a symbol of royalty, greatness and sophistication, and although the energies of the cheetah are 'tamer' than the other big cats, it should not be treated with any less respect. Their energy is surrounding swiftness and speed - albeit in short bursts - and useful if you wish to have a magical working that needs to carry a swift message. The cheetah is different from all the other felines. Although they are the easiest of the big cats to domesticate they are still wild animals and have a pretty fierce bite. This consideration needs to be taken while working magically with this element of cat-power. If shape shifting, the anatomy of the cheetah also needs special consideration as their claws are not retractable, which enables them to run at the speeds they do and stops them from slipping. I would give them the Element of Air for their swiftness and ability to carry messages (and whatever else) at top speed.

Cougar or Puma *(puma concolot)*

This cat is known under many names such as mountain cat, mountain lion, puma, catamount and even panther - actually holding the record for the most names to be held by an individual cat species. It has a very wide range from Canada to the Andes, and has the biggest range of any terrestrial mammal in the western hemisphere.

A member of the *Felid* species and the second heaviest of the cats in America, they are a tawny colour but can be grey or reddish depending on their location and age. They all have a lighter fur on the underbelly jaws and chin; and are born spotted with a ring on the tail. They are slender with a round head but with muscular back legs and large feet to match. The large neck and jaws are extremely powerful so they can hold down their prey. They do not roar but make the same purring and lower growling noise like the domestic cats.

In the Inca Mysteries it is said that the cougar was one of the animal symbols of Viracocha, who was elevated to national sun-deity status. He was said to have come from Lake Titicaca to create man-statues, which he brought to life before returning back into the water from where he came. His attendants, who were classed as minor deities, were depicted in the shape of a cougar, falcon, snake and condor, and represented him among mankind when he went back into the waters.

In Bolivia there is an ancient temple complex called Pumapanka sometimes called 'Puma Pancha' or 'Puma Puncha'. The impressive gateway is known as the 'door of the cougar'. There is a mystery surrounding the building of the structure as the technology that was used in building the complex did not match the evolutionary stage of the people at that time, even though this theme of the cougar was represented at the ancient cities throughout South America. Cuzco is an ancient city where the whole town is shaped into that of the cougar. The Cochiti Indians of New Mexico would carve life sized statues of the cougar and erect temples to honour them. Remnants of this can still be seen in the ruins today. Here is the evidence of the cougar being held in high esteem by the ancient tribes and its link to their deity Viracocha their great father deity.

In Native American culture, the Apache and Wallapi people believed that the cry of the cougar was a harbinger of death, while the Great Lake tribes believed their tails could whip up the waves of the lakes. The cougar was so revered by some tribes in Southern California that they would neither kill the animal, nor protect their livestock from it. The Cherokee tribe called them 'Klandagi', which means lord of the forest. Its cat-power denotes power, leadership and swiftness, which are attributes of the animal itself for although the cougar is another 'stalk and ambush' creature, it is an extremely swift animal in the chase.

Magic attributes

The magical attributes of great strength and swiftness are best associated with the cougar. We must not forget that it was revered by the ancient people of America as having great powers of destruction and as a bringer of storms - though we should not ignore the paternal protective character that these creatures represent. The cougar as a power animal represents the primal energy of male and the Element of Water in the guise of the dark waters of the storm and deadly rivers. The energies of this power animal are ferocious and fierce and should not be used lightly, and while protective and good to have around for strength in battle it can also be destructive if not moderated. However we should also consider that the rains and storms that bring darkness and destruction are the rains to sustain life and fertility for the land and for its people.

Lynx (*pardinus* Iberian; *canadensis* Canadian; *lynx lynx* Siberian)

The lynx is a medium sized wild cat and its name is derived from the Greek *lunx*, and the Indo-European word *leuk*, which means 'light brightness' after the startling brilliance of its eyes. The animal is very hardy with varying species found in Canada, North America, Northern Europe, Siberia and the peninsula of Iberia. The Iberian lynx is the most critically endangered of all. According to the conservation group SOS Lynx if this species died out then it would be the first feline extinction since the *smilodon* (the sabre-toothed cat) around 10,000 years ago. The Canadian lynx has a thicker coat and paws, and is much stronger in order to support itself in the snow and make its home in sheltered trees and rocks. The Eurasian lynx is the biggest of the family and the national emblem of Macedonia and Romania.

Lynx have short tails and tufts of black hair on the ears, with a ruff on the neck that resembles a bow tie. They range from medium brown to a pale gold colour; sometimes with small brown spots with white hair on the chest, belly and the inside of the legs. The size and height varies within their climate range. The lynx although solitary will travel and hunt in groups and prefers covered forest areas with a lot of grass to enable it to remain hidden; although they are very adept at climbing trees and extremely good swimmers.

They are one of the few members of the cat family which likes water and fish as part of their diet. Their stealth has led them to be associated with the mystical ghost-like behaviour of seeing without being seen, combined with their bright eyes which were said to be able to see through trees and rocks and even underground.

Magical attributes

If journeying on a path working or meditation, listen and follow the lynx as it will lead you to what you wish to know - whether this information be in a symbolic form or a direct answer. Associated with the power of invisibility and with its keen sight, the lynx.is able to see deeper into anything physical and otherworldly. This sight may be developed within us to see deep into the psyche not just of others we come into contact with but also within ourselves.

European Wild Cat *(felis silvestus)*

Considered to be one of the oldest of its species. This forest cat was widespread throughout Europe and the Mediterranean but due to hunting and human habitation is now only found in small pockets of Scotland, mainland Europe and the Mediterranean. Thought to be one of the fore runners of our domestic cat, with markings similar to a tabby, though not as spaced out. Its colour range can be from mid brown to grey depending on the location. The size compared to a domestic cat is similar but it has a broader head and shorter tail. Its coat tends to be longish in length.

Those who liken the Scottish wild cat to the domestic tabby are deceived. They are similar in appearance but that is as far as it goes. While it is thought that the wild cat did mate with some domestic cats to produce the similarities in appearance there is one noticeable difference. As Mélusine Draco puts it in *Traditional Witchcraft for Urban Living*, there is evidence that wild cats have mated with domestic cats and domestic cats can survive in the wild having gone feral, but they don't usually move far from human habitation and will quickly revert if given the opportunity. The wild cat however cannot be handled or tamed; even as a small kitten it is extremely ferocious.

In Scotland the wild cat was used on crests such as the Clan Mackintosh, which features a feisty-looking cat, with the motto "Touch not the cat bot (*bot* meaning 'without') a glove"; and for the Clan MacGillivray the motto is "Touch not this cat". The wildcat was also a totem of a number of other early Celtic and Pictish tribes and its symbol is of strength, courage and leadership.

Magical attributes

The ferocious magical nature cannot be tamed, so be wary if wishing to work with this power animal. Wild cats are associated in folklore with the 'fairy fold' and have the ability to answer questions if they can be tempted. They are also guardians of earthly treasure. The mating cries were associated with many folk stories and the harbinger of omens. Because of their ability to survive in some of the coldest areas of northern countries I will assign their Element as Earth and the dark brooding nature of the darker and fiercer nature of the human psyche. Those are the emotions that are difficult to control: such as anger, hate and violence, which are associated usually with fire. IF you get close enough to the wild cat to see the facial expression the aura is one of 'back off and beware'. The ancient Clans used to fight like with like, and the symbol of the wildcat was based on strength and fighting ability, with protection for the clan and land. Bear in mind these Scottish tribes were some of the toughest adversaries to come across and the Romans for all their great legions built Hadrian's Wall to keep them out! The magical attributes for this cat are linked somewhat with the domestic cat but somewhat fiercer: fierce protective energies especially within family and community situations.

Power or Totem Animals

A power or totem animal in modern parlance appears to be a bit blurred as to its meaning: **it is an animal that has a close association with a particular person, tribe, group or clan.** The animal usually chooses the individual not the other way around. There are certain individuals who claim their totem or power animals as being a wolf - an animal of choice for those who have an interest in shamanism. Often these people are vegetarians who do not like killing of any kind - even in Nature. This is unbelievable since the animal *has* to suit the individual's underlying personality (wolves are pack hunters and can be very aggressive), and reveals that their choice is more of a flight of fancy rather than self-discovery.

Sometimes the power animal that reveals itself is not exactly what we would choose. One friend, who is genuinely a follower of the shamanistic path, has told me that when she was a beginner, the group performed an exercise to find their own personal animals. While she was hoping for something large and impressive, she ended up with a badger; while another student discovered hers was a frog! Both, however, realised how comfortably they each 'fitted' with these creatures, and what these animal guides have to show them.

The witch and her traditional familiarity with the cat does not necessarily mean a totem or power animal, but possibly a familiar with whom they share a psychic connection, or simply a family pet. Some witches have dogs that act as familiars, warning of any trouble in a way that only a witch would understand. It is also possible to connect with them and see things through their eyes on a psychic level. A witch knows the behaviour of their animal companions inside and out, knowing that certain twitches and movements are responses when asked a certain question. The partnership is a close one of friendship as well as a working magical one.

Folklore abounds with stories of witches being able to shapeshift into the bodies of cats, owls, bats or foxes - but performing this is not necessarily a *physical* manifestation into the animal's shape. In many cases it is performed on another level entirely by invoking the spirit of the particular animal that we wish to become, and projecting this image to another location. From ancient times, many cultures achieved this by wearing masks of the animals and performing ritual dances to invoke the spirit; as well as wearing the skins, bones and even the actual heads of the animals, believing this would help them harness the strength and energy of the totem or power creature.

In Sir James Frazer's *Golden Bough* he cites a story about a South Africa tribe, whose group soul was linked to a cat. One of the daughters had married a man of a neighbouring tribe and as she was leaving she wanted to take the cat with her. The family offered her other animals as a parting gift but she refused and took the cat. She kept it confined so no one would find it but one day when she was out working in the fields, the cat escaped and put on the war attire of the husband and started to dance and sing in the house. A group of children heard the racket and decided to investigate. The cat started to make fun of the children and became abusive so they ran and told the husband who came to see what all the fuss was about. When he discovered the cat he asked what it was doing but the cat started to abuse him, too. The husband became very angry and killed the cat, at which point the wife who was in the field collapsed. She had enough strength to ask her husband to take the cat back home. The cat was wrapped in a mat and taken back to the wife's tribe and when it was unwrapped, all the people of village dropped down dead. That was the end of the tribe of the cat.

The Butuk tribe believe they have three souls, with one of them being external and living in a particular animal. If that animal is killed then the individual will die. Tribes named after a particular animal was not native just to Africa. In Britain, for example, surnames names such as Lamb, Fox and Bird are thought to be tribal in origin. Native American cultures have used animals such as the cougar and jaguar in a shamanic context; while the Aboriginal Australians (where felines are not part of their fauna) have great respect for their desert creatures and used them as power animals in shamanic rituals.

Stepping Into Circle

To discover your own power animal try the following exercise but keep an open mind as this may not be what you expect it to be.

- Find a time when you will not be disturbed. Switch off all phones and alarms or anything that may go off and disturb you. Ensure you are wearing comfortable clothing and are relaxed.
- Find a space where you can draw your magic Circle. It is best to work within Circle as this is the area where the magical energy is concentrated.

- Prepare the Circle according to your tradition and sit comfortably facing North. Close your eyes and take deep slow breaths. If you want to use a personal chant to call the relevant spirit that is fine. You can make it as simple or elaborate as you wish, however the most simple of calls can be just as effective such as this one:

Animal spirit join me here.
I call you to my side.
I call the one who walks with me.
My animal spirit guide.

- Wait to see what happens. See what psychic signs filter through from your subconscious. These can be subtle or a full blown experience. If you do not get a result first time don't worry you can try again another time. Sometimes they may appear when you least expect it - like while doing the washing up, or walking to work. The experience is different for everyone.
- When you think you have finished, close the Circle down according to your tradition.
- It is always wise to keep a record in your magical journal.

Herbal Exercise

Tiger balm is used to sooth sore and aching muscles as well as being placed on pressure points at the base of the neck and temples to relieve headaches and calm tension. A homemade version is easy to make. You will need.

15g of beeswax.
60ml of extra virgin olive oil.
10 drops of peppermint oil.
10 drops of eucalyptus oil.
6 drops of clove oil.

Glass jar for storing.

A double boiler or a large saucepan of hot water with a smaller heat-proof dish inside.

Method

Place the bowl in the saucepan of hot water and heat the beeswax and the oil together in the bowl. Add the oils to the mixture and stir. Remove from the heat and safely pour the contents of the bowl into the glass jar and allow to cool. Store in a cool dark place and use within 12 months.

PART TWO

The Domestic Cat

Cats sleep anywhere, any table, any chair.
Top of piano, window-ledge, in the middle, on the edge.
Open draw, empty shoe, anybody's lap will do.
Fitted in a cardboard box, in the cupboard with your frocks.
Anywhere! They don't care! Cats sleep anywhere.
Eleanor Farjeon, Cats Sleep Anywhere

The small *felis libyca,* a light tabby African wild cat, native to areas bordering the Mediterranean, and the ring-tailed cat *felis chaus,* which was thought to be from the Middle East, are believed to be the original species domesticated by the ancient Egyptians. These small cats found easy pickings in the mice and rats running around the grain supplies, and as cats have always had this instinctive ability to find good sources of food, the great Egyptian grain stores were an attractive prospect.

The Egyptians realised this and encouraged the cats as in ancient times there were no sophisticated farming and storing method, to protect the food stores and make sure there was enough to eat. It was not long before these animals forged a bond with humans and became much-loved members of the family. If a cat died, it was mourned, mummified and given the appropriate funerary rites. Cats had become so sacred to the Egyptians that the people guarded them jealously, which led to other cultures like the Greeks smuggling them on board their trade ships as vermin controllers. This was an illegal act in Egyptian law and society; anyone caught stealing or harming a cat would be sentenced to death.

The European wild cat (*felis silvestus*) with its distinctive rounded black tail, may also have added to the gene pool of the modern domestic cat; while the fourth contender is Pallas's cat (*felis manul*), which could be the origin of our long-haired breeds.

Domestic cats are the second most popular of pets but those who think they own a cat are pretty much mistaken. Unlike the dog, who is generally obedient and faithful to its owner, the cat remains an independent and aloof creature. By nature they are solitary: unlike dogs who are pack animals. Cats only want to know you on their terms, but they do have a habit of being able to tune into the emotions of humans. Cats are creatures of routine and get upset when that routine is broken. Nevertheless, they are capable of adapting their lifestyle to suit themselves. When an owner dies they do not pine but quickly adapt to other surroundings and even new owners. If this were not the case then their species would not have survived as long as they have.

The Senses of a Power Animal

A cat's ability to predict the weather has attracted many superstitions. It was believed that witches who rode the storm took the form of a cat. While in America if a cat sits with its back to the fire then we are heading for a cold snap; the same is said if a cat sleeps with all four paws tucked under its body. If they wash inside and around their ears, then rain will be upon us within the day or most certainly the next. An old rhyme by Dr Eresmus Darwin goes:

Puss on the hearth with velvet paws.
Sits wiping o'er her whiskered jaws,
twill surely rain, I see with sorrow,
our jaunt must be put off tomorrow.

This sensitivity could be due to membranes in the ear that are able to pick up changes in the atmosphere. Cats can also turn their ears around 180 degrees, because they have 32 muscles in each ear that can move over ten times faster than any dog's. These muscles also help them to hear sounds from more than one direction at any given time up to a metre away. Their lowest hearing range is around 30 KHZ around thirty cycles per second (which is about the same as humans) but the highest is 65 KHZ, which is sixty five thousand cycles per second! This means they can hear the high-pitched squeaks of prey, and for a mother to hear the call of a kitten from a distance. This may explain why cats respond to women and children's voices more readily than to a male voice, as the pitch of the voice is higher.

A cat's ears when alert are pricked. If they are really listening, trying to locate a source of sound, their ears will pull forward and rotate to the source of the sound's direction.

When they are upset or frightened they go flat to their head. This is a mechanism that also helps protect their ears when they are fighting. Cat-napping means appearing to be half asleep whilst being fully aware of what is going on around them. But even asleep, cats are alert to any sound that is out of the ordinary.

Their eyes are adapted for hunting with them being placed looking straight ahead and large in comparison to their skull. This way they have stereoscopic vision, unlike other animals which can see a different picture from each eye. This helps cats to see and judge distances very well, and the less they move the less chance they have of being detected. They are also able to detect objects at a distance but have difficulty focusing on stationary objects. The muscles in the iris expand and contract in different types of light, in the daytime they are slits to protect the inner eye from sunlight, but at night they are opened up wide to allow them to make use of whatever light is available. Cats are nocturnal hunters by nature but cannot see in total darkness. Their eyes utilize all the light that comes into them with the *topedum lucidum*: meaning 'bright carpet' - a layer over the eye that reflects the light back onto the retina. This inspired Percy Shaw to name his invention 'cats eyes' - those reflective light beads that are seen world-wide in the centre of the road at night.

The sense of smell in a cat is probably the most important of all. In kittens it develops very early and as they grow it becomes much stronger, helping them to map out their surroundings. A cat always smells anything before deciding if it is of any use to them. Watch a cat with a bowl of food - because it always has a good sniff to make sure it's up to its culinary standards! The sense of smell is linked to the taste buds, if a cat is unwell and cannot smell its food, it will not eat.

While walking their territory, cats also sniff around the boundaries to see who has been there and marked their territory. They rub themselves on fences, walls, on the grass, paths and even on humans to show that this territory belongs to them: Keep Out. On the other hand, the covering of their faeces is the opposite of being territorial. It is a mark of protection to prevent predators from picking up a scent and finding their den, especially when a mother needs to keep her kittens safe. So, as well as leaving their scent, they are quite capable of concealing where they have been as well.

Magical attributes

The magical attributes of the domestic cat are lunar and feminine in their vibrations, with the qualities of the maternal nurturing mother and protector of her family. In this guise she has a more mellow temperament than the other power animals of the feline family. Her energy is kind, gentle, welcoming and comforting. Cat-power embraces love, fertility and sexual promiscuity; the lunar power of attraction has a strong and seductive sexual nature. Great care should be harnessed when using this force as it can be very intense and with an added influence of the Moon the outcome is unpredictable - for ill or good. Cat-power also influences creativity and the arts in all of its forms: whether home improvement, dance, fashion, music and anything that has the potential for creating something beautiful and/or entertaining.

For those who wish to embrace the domestic cat as a power

animal, we also need to remember that these creatures are still hunters and it is in the animal's biological nature. Even our domestic pets will go out and kill a bird or small rodent ... not necessarily to eat but to bring home a source of food to support the family and this is inherent in their DNA. Let's make no bones about it: domestic cats are fiercely independent and never fully domesticated: they remain a law unto themselves.

Feral Cats

Not all cats are domesticated. In many counties all over the world cats are working animals just as they were before the Egyptians encouraged them into their homes. These animals have adapted to living semi-wild, catching their own food and wary of anything that might cause a threat to them including humans. They often become barn or factory cats, catching mice and keeping the vermin population under control for a daily handout of food. There are an estimated one million feral cats in the UK alone, and it is a testimony to their ability for adaptation and survival in any environment. Some cats are naturally feral and prefer freedom and independence; others become feral through no fault of their own, having either become lost or abandoned by their owners. Generally, feral cats can re-adapt to home comforts but some, due to their conditioning, remain wild and untameable. Others have had traumatic experiences and take a while to trust humans again before being comfortable with them.

Magical attributes

To use a feral cat as a power animal would be a quite interesting choice! These energies are in keeping with those of the domestic cat, with planetary energies and symbols remaining the same - but with a wilder and more aggressive nature. The magical attributes are those of cunning and stealth to survive; these hunting instincts and abilities are more finely tuned as they are defined by the natural order of survival of the fittest - not just hunting for play or sport.

Stepping Into Circle

One way of being mindful of just how a cat's world feels, pay attention to those smells that we register but just don't think about. Like waking on a summer morning and smelling air perfumed by flowers, or if it has been raining, the smell of wet pavements. Or walking past a local Costa and getting that homely smell of ground coffee beans. Or passing a pub where you can smell the stale smell of beer – but also knowing there is a thirst-quenching pint of lager if you popped in.

There are two ways of heightening these sensations, depending on how potent you want your senses to react. Firstly, you can either go for a walk or potter around in the garden and see how many different types of smell you can detect, and try to identify them. It can be surprising just what you can identify with conscious thought, since most of the time our minds are elsewhere and taking these things for granted.

This next point may sound silly but it is a way of getting another perspective, and the idea came from a workplace experiment. I've had poor sight all my life, so my other senses overcompensate to make up for the shortfall. The company I work for wanted a better understanding of people with 'sensory disabilities' and how that had an impact on day to day living.

One person wearing a blindfold had another guiding them around the store for about twenty minutes, both participants taking it in turns to wear the blindfold. On completion of the exercise, the data was gathered and it was found that while they were blindfolded the individual, who felt a little vulnerable at first, began to use the other senses at their disposal. Gradually they began to use their sense of smell to identify certain areas of the work place; the more they did this the more they managed to create a type of 'scent map'. If you are willing to go to the trouble to perform this experiment, enlist the help of someone who is willing to participate. Or you can simply try just walking around with your eyes blindfolded, provided it is safe and you won't fall over things in the house or garden.

The above experiment can also be used to gain another insight on how the world appears from a cat's perspective of hearing.

Although we do not have a cat's superior hearing abilities, if we concentrate we can distinguish different sounds, the direction it is coming from, and how far away we think it is. In other words, we become more aware of air currents and different directions of the breeze and wind. We don't have the ability like the cat to rotate our ears but we can fine-tune our own senses to pick up sounds on different wavelengths.

On a deeper level, these experiments will help us recognise things on a more subtle level, and if we get *really* good at it we will be able to sense things on different atmospheric frequencies. It is something our primitive ancestors were able to do - an ability we have lost over time. **This instinct can be linked to the so-called sixth sense that some humans possess quite naturally. It is also the first step to entering the domain of cat-power.**

Herbal Exercise

Pussy Willow

The pussy willow is a member of the smaller willow, *salix* family, and those interested in cat-power might want to have a tree in their garden - not just for its magical properties but also for its healing abilities. The male grey willow before flowering has buds of greyish fluffy heads which look like tiny cats - hence the name pussy willow - which turn into rose coloured buds and flowers of purple or orange. This is the one to grow. The trees are hardy and don't mind a lot of pruning but need controlling as they can take over a garden; they dislike the shade and like most soils but it must be moist.

Traditionally and magically, the willow is associated with the moon, the Element of Water, deep emotion, femininity, fertility (the speed it can grow), and motherhood: all associations of the cat. The time of the willow is in the early spring from when life shoots forth from the womb, and when Bast, the Egyptian cat-goddess, had her festival to mark the spring as a time of fertility.

Part Three

The Great Cat Gods of Egypt

When a person can stand upon a high place, under the bright sun and exalt at being alive, and in the flesh and almost drunk with it all, clenching his fists in unconscious use of ka posture, then it is Sekhmet which roars within.

[*The Inner guide to Egypt*, Alan Richardson and B Walker John]

The ancient Egyptians had a very rich history in the recognition of cat-power and by the Middle Kingdom, domestic cats had been deified in the form of the homely Bastet. There is also a considerable amount of evidence from archaeological finds that support the use of feline symbolism in the Egyptian religious system and, as we have already discussed, can be found in the tombs, writings, statues and the large number of mummified cats discovered in excavations.

The Egyptians identified with the animals around them and related their attributes to the deities they worshipped: often expressed in images of the head of a particular animal with the body of a human. The Egyptians were also aware of the duality of nature and the multi-faceted aspects of these powers; especially those represented by the lion and the cat, which were widely used and interchangeable with each other.

Atum-Re

All the father-creator gods of Egypt have been associated with the Great Sphinx - one of the oldest and most famous lion monuments in the world to be found at Giza on the west bank of the Nile. This large monolithic statue, standing at 241 feet long, 20 feet wide and 25 feet high, is said to date from the early Pyramid Age, and has the body of a lion and the head of a crowned man. Nevertheless, geological research based on the erosion of the body suggests that it is not just wind and sand damage that could have aged the monument - evidence on the rock suggests water damage. Robert M Schoch, Professor of Natural Science at Boston University has studied the structure and concludes that erosion shows a period of significant rainfall and the last period in history where the region saw that amount of rainfall was the fourth millennia BC!

The body of the Sphinx is made of a separate limestone to that of the head; the head, which is a harder limestone, suggests restoration in the Fourth Dynasty. Samples taken from the stone for testing caused speculation by suggesting that the head is much newer than the body. Margaret Murry in *The Splendour That Was Egypt* writes:

> The sphinx as a portrait statue becomes common in the Middle Kingdom. Though known before as a composite animal with a lion's body and a falcon's or a ram's head. It is only in this period that it first becomes a portrait of the monarch the lion's body is still retained, but the face is human with the lion's mane surrounding it, rather later the whole head is represented as human.

What we do know is that the Egyptians regarded the Sphinx as a guardian between our world and that of the darkness of night - the Otherworld. The monument faced due east towards the direction of the rising sun. The rising of the sun heralds the rebirth of the sun-god Re, after his perilous journey through the Underworld on the boat of millions of years, having slain the demon of darkness, the great snake Apothis.

Magical attributes, invocation or charm for Atum-Re

Hail to you Re, on your rising,
and to you Aten, on your setting,

you rise every day, shine brightly every day,
while you appear in glory, king of the gods.
You are lord of the sky and lord of the earth,
who have created the creatures above and those below.
[Book of the Dead - Chapter 15]

Aker

The guardian of the east and western portals is thought to be a representation of the god Aker, usually represented by two sets of front paws of lions or two lions facing away from each other. A much more primitive version of Aker was a group of deities known as the Akru, who would savage anyone on the Underworld path except for the king who, in ancient times, was the only one granted access. Here we see a dual representation of the forces not just governing the solar day where Re is the creative force, but also the forces of night and the Underworld where the deity protects those who have permission to pass through the realms.

Magical attributes, invocation or charm for Aker

The dual lion-god can be petitioned to act as a guardian for the Adept who passes through the Underworld as part of his initiation. This invocation is to be performed at dawn or dusk - the time of transition when the doors to the Otherworld open to allow Amun Re and his barque access into and out of these realms. Contacting the spirits and ancestors from the Otherworld for answers to our questions is not to be undertaken lightly since a true answer may be not what we want to hear.

- Prepare your Circle in accordance to your tradition.
- In the Circle you will need: a lamp, either of the oil burning type, or one that carries a tea light. A burner of opium incense, or joss sticks - whichever you prefer to use.
- Settle down facing east at dawn, or west at dusk.

- When you are ready and focused chant the invocation.
  The spirits of the dead let them tell me the truth to-day in that
  about which I ask for I am Aker guardian of the eastern and
  western door way. Come in to me Anubis with thy fair face. I
  have come to pray to thee. South, north, east and west, every
  breeze of Amenti. Let them come into being.

- Gaze into the flame of the lamp and watch what happens.

See what results you get from this exercise and when it is over
close down your Circle and record anything you see in your
journal, even a small detail that might seem insignificant at the
time … the reason may make itself known at another time.

Amun and Mut

Amun was a local deity of Thebes but by the Middle Kingdom he
had been elevated to supreme solar deity, although his cult centre
still remained in the city of Thebes. Although his worship was of
the higher spiritual path of the Egyptian Mysteries, Amun
remained a popular deity and was given the title: 'fierce red-eyed
lion'. As well as invoking the lion-goddess Sekhmet, the king
would also appeal to Amun-Re to help smite his enemies.

Amun wore a circlet crown with two large plumes that were
divided to represent the Egyptian concept of duality. His sacred
animal was the curved horned ram, although both ram and lion
were combined in the sphinx statues of the New Kingdom to give
the body of a lion and the head of a ram. His consort was Mut,
who also bore the attributes of a lioness and is sometimes
depicted as having a head of a lioness. This is when Mut is in her
warlike mode - defender of the children of Egypt. There is
sometimes a blurred line between Mut and Sekhmet and indeed
the similarities in nature are very close.

In her calmer image when she was more approachable and
could be stroked, she was likened to the cat-goddess Bastet, when

she was known as Mut-Bastet. The Mut-Bastet duality is typical of the Egyptian concept of belief, since they represented both sides of the forces of nature with its beneficial and harmful effects from the energy that was invoked.

Magical attributes, invocation or charm for Amun and Mut

Amun can be petitioned for the invigorating energy brought by the sun, while his consort Mut is called upon in her capacity as the Great Mother.

Mut: *Homage to thee, O Sekhmet-Bast-Re, thou mistress of the gods*
Amun: *This holy god, the lord of all the gods, Amun-Re,*
The lord of the throne of the two lands

Bastet

No other culture showed more respect and love for the cat than the ancient Egyptians, even deifying them in the name of Bastet, the alter ego of the lioness but in a softer form becoming the goddess of motherhood, joy, pleasure, music and fertility. Cats became so sacred that the people guarded them jealously.

Bastet (Bast) was originally a local deity of Bubastis but was later elevated to national status when thousands of pilgrims gathered for her annual festival, which, according to Herodotus, was a huge orgiastic celebration of feasting on wine, food and song. This was celebrating the promiscuous fertility aspect of Bastet's nature, which was closely linked with the behaviour of the female cat when she is in season. Women who wanted to get pregnant would carry a talisman of Bastet in the hope that it would give them power to conceive.

The origin of her name is still uncertain but her hieroglyph is a perfume jar with her name next to it. In appearance she was a cat-headed woman; in her right hand she carries a sistrum, a musical instrument that is a type of rattle that suggests her association with music, dance and the arts - an association she shares with Hathor. In her other hand she holds the aegis of Bastet: a head of a lioness with a wide, half circle necklace – she also carries a bag over one shoulder.

Within her temple complex at Leontopolis ('lion city') was a sanctuary of the lion-god Mihos, who was said to be Bastet's son. The temple was set lower than the town surrounded by trees, which gave it the appearance of an island, and in the centre was a large statue of Bastet, in the temple grounds were multitudes of cats that were cared for by the priesthood. Omens used to be concluded by the movements or slightest tail twitches from these animals and on their death, they were buried with great honour and mummification just like humans. It was illegal to kill a cat with the penalty of death if an individual was found guilty. It was also illegal to take a cat out of the country but as Bubastis was on a main trading route of the Nile, some either crept on-board ships, or were smuggled out by Greek traders who saw their worth as pest controllers. The Egyptian word for cat was *meow*, which is in keeping with their vocal sounds.

Magical attributes, invocation or charm for Bastet

Cats like humans and other animals are very protective of their young; as the people of Egypt were identified as her children so she became protector of the people. Bastet shows the softer side of the feline nature - that of protector, nurturer and all aspects of motherhood as well as being mistress of music, dance and the arts, and all aspects of love and beauty. She was also associated with the elements and attributes of healing. She can be petitioned for any help in the area of a creative block, or those things with an outward expression of creativity and beauty, and those aspects beneficial to the home. She is the deity of women and patron of marriage.

This spell is from the *Egyptian Book of Days* by Melusine Draco and is a prayer/ invocation to Bastet.

I am she who is called Divine amongst women.
For me was built the city of Bubastis.
I brought together woman and man.
I burdened woman with the new borne babe in the tenth month.
I ordained that parents should be beloved by their children.
I inflict retribution on those that feel no love for their parents.
I compelled woman to be loved by man.
I found out marriage contracts for women.

Bes

The dwarf god Bes is not really a feline deity, although his short, squat body is always depicted wearing a panther skin and with the attributes of the lion being found in the mane that surrounds his face and the tail. He ferociously wields swords and his prime task is to protect children and women, especially those in pregnancy and labour. His fierce persona also wards off evil spirits, demons, poisonous and dangerous creatures, and insects that may invade the home. At night carvings and statues were placed in the bedroom; headrests adorned with carvings of Bes were thought to ward off bad dreams.

He was not just a benevolent god who fought off evil. He came to be seen as a jovial character who jumped and danced around. In late Egyptian history he was depicted as dancing and playing the tambourine, entertaining Hathor with his merriment. Ladies' mirrors, makeup boxes and kohl compacts were decorated with images of Bes in order to act as a stimulus for sexual feelings and promote fertility in couples.

Magical attributes, invocation or charm for Bes

You protect me against all the wild beasts of the desert.
All the crocodiles of the river.
All the snakes and the scorpions.
All the insects that bite with their mandibles and sting with their
*   tails.*

All the types of reptiles that attack in their caves.

Sekhmet

The lion-goddess Sekhmet is the deity of war, famine and destruction – and one of the older, more primitive deities. During the hot summer days, just before the Inundation of the Nile, when the river was at its lowest, people and animals braced themselves as this period before the flood often brought disease and death – referred to as 'the arrows of Sekhmet'.

To protect against these deadly 'arrows', it was necessary to recite a spell from *The Book of the Last Days of the Year* over a piece of linen cloth which was to be tied around the neck of the individual to be protected. So feared was this goddess that on New Years Day amulets were exchanged as gifts of Sekhmet (or her alter ego Bastet), to appease her and prevent any suffering during the following year. In rituals to honour the gods in the New Year celebrations, Sekhmet would play a very big role in being honoured and asked to protect Pharaoh, the people, and the land from enemies, death, famine, disease, even the dangers of flies. The list for her assistance in the protection of the state was indeed a very long one.

One well-known tale is that of Atum, who retreats to the heavens tired and unhappy that mankind is plotting against him and sends the 'Eye of Re' to punish them. Once Sekhmet gets started, she kills and drinks the blood of humanity, retiring in the evening only to start again the next day. She does not stop and threatens to destroy humanity all together. The gods became concerned and flooded the land with beer, stained with pomegranate juice. Next morning Sekhmet ready and hungry for more killing sees the red liquid and thinking it to be blood begins to drink. She gets so drunk, completely forgets what she is doing and returns home. Humanity is saved from ultimate destruction.

Sekhmet is a force to be reckoned with but as with all ancient Egyptian magic, this power although harmful could also be beneficial. Pharaoh would take the spirit of Sekhmet into battle to be sure of victory against the enemies of Egypt. In Memphis, however, the priesthood of Sekhmet's temple specialised as doctors and she was regarded as the patron of surgeons. The Egyptians were the most advanced ancient culture skilled in the art of healing and surgery and believed in fighting like with like. So although Sekhment was an untameable force going up against demons that caused an illness, she was also a powerful healing deity.

Magical attributes, invocation or charm for Sekhmet

Sekhmet's energy is that of intense solar power and there is no soft side to this force. She like the Hindu goddess Kali, represented the darker side of the feminine nature. She represented death and destruction to make way for a new beginning. Sekhmet can represent raw power unleashed; unable to be controlled, much like Kali who when in a state of rage trampled her husband Shiva into the ground killing him, not realising what she had done until afterwards when it was too late. The energy that Sekhmet wields should not be viewed as bad or evil. It is a *natural* energy that when used respectfully can be beneficial, but it is one force that should not be used indiscriminately.

This spell for Sekhmet uses 'the nine bows' as a curse against enemies. From the *Ancient Egyptian Literature vol 1 The Old and Middle Kingdom* by Miriam Lichtheim Taken from the Middle Kingdom Period from a 'Cycle of Hymms To King Ssestostris 3rd'.

Hail to you, Khakaure, our Horus, divine of form.
Lands protector who widens its borders.
Who smites foreign countries with his crown.
Who holds the two lands in his arms embrace.
Who subdues foreign lands by a motion of his hands.
Who slays bowmen without a blow from a club.

Shoots the arrows without drawing the string.
Whose terror strikes the bowmen in their land.
Fear of whom smites the nine bows.
Whose slaughter brought death to thousands of bowmen.
[who had come] to invade his borders.
Who shoots the arrow as does Sekhmet ...
... He is Sekhmet to foes who tread on his frontier!

Shu and Tefnut

Shu, the god of dry air who, together with his sister-consort, goddess of moist air Tefnut, were the first offspring born of Atum. Shu and Tefnut are represented by lions – whose symbol was also two lions back to back. They had a sanctuary at Heliopolis, where Tefnut also represented the 'Eye of Re'.

One myth tells of how the Eye of Re (Tefnut) went south into Nubia (modern Sudan) and dwelt there in the desert as a lioness (or wild cat) after a fit of temper. Re who wanted her back - as she was his divine protector - sent an envoy, which in the early texts was Shu, but later the role fell on Thoth. The envoy persuaded her to return by telling her fables of Egypt which continued for the rest of the journey home. When she returned and was reunited with her father, she was transformed into the goddess Sekhmet, who became his left eye and fierce protector of her father.

Magical attributes, invocation or charm for Shu and Tefnut

Tefnut is a mother-creator goddess and her attribute is the moisture that creates life. This energy can be quite intense and brooding, which can be found in the darker side of the female personality. She can also be identified with the 'crone of wisdom' and as one of the oldest of the deities represents the dark of the moon.

You have your offering-bread O Atum and Ruti
Who yourselves created your godheads and your persons,
O Shu and Tefnut who made the gods.
Who begot the gods and established the gods.
[Pyramid Texts: Utterance 301,147]

This verse shows Shu and Tefnut as the children of Atum, the supreme creator. The reference to Ruti (literally meaning 'two lions') is thought to be Aker under another name.

Stepping Into Circle: Meditation

The Tarot card 'Strength' is the representation of Bastet and her energies and that of her sister Sekhmet. Here, however, we are only going to concentrate on the gentler energies of Bastet. You will need the card Strength, and a statue or picture of Bastet. If you wish you can light a candle and/or incense of the appropriate colour and blend.

- Find a time when you are not going to be disturbed.
- Prepare a circle according to your tradition.
- Sit quietly with the Tarot card in front of you and meditate on the image.
- How did you feel?
- What feel did you get for the energies?
- Was there anything that stood out for you?

Record any impressions that you received from this exercise in your magical journal as it will be useful at a later date when we do this experiment again.

Herbal Exercise

Cats claw (*uncaria ttomentosa*) is a herb native to areas of South America, the name deriving from the long thorns on its leaves that look like cats' claws. It is grown in the damp regions of the

Amazonian rain forests and for thousands of years the Native Indian tribes, especially those of Peru, have used the bark and roots for their amazing healing abilities. The shaman of the tribes believed the plant harboured good spirits and would use parts of it in their medicines. Although it has no associations with ancient Egypt, it is still an effective magical property when summoning cat-power.

In contemporary medicine it is used to aid digestive problems, arthritis, inflammation, ulcers and to encourage the healing of wounds, as well as boosting the immune system since it contains antioxidants that get rid of cell-damaging free radicals. The plant is now thought to contain powerful alkaloids that can combat disease and research being carried out on the beneficial uses against diseases such as Crohn's disease, HIV and certain cancers. Magically, used alone or with other herbs, cat's claw is beneficial for protection, prosperity and money drawing.

To Make A Cat's Claw Protective Pouch

You will need a small white, string pouch, which can be made or purchased from any retail outlet or online. Inside place some root or bark of cat's claw and some dragon's blood resin. If you really want to make it more potent you can actually add a discarded claw of a cat, as this will enhance the power of the charm. Seal the bag and hang it over the threshold, dashboard of a car, or carry it on your person as a protective charm.

Money drawing

This is pretty much the same as the above with just some slight amendments. This time you will need a green bag. Add to the bag cat's claw herb with basil leaves, as basil has been used to attract business success and prosperity for many years. You can also place in the bag a silver coin as this is an old gypsy charm to aid prosperity. Hang the bag over the threshold to attract good financial success, or carry it about your person.

PART FOUR

Superstition

The cat as the seer in the darkness is a zoomorphic emblem, as
the moon is a celestial emblem of an identical principle.
[Kenneth Grant, *Aleister Crowley and the Hidden God*.]

Over the centuries cats have been the subject of superstition regarding good or bad luck depending on which country we are from, and even what region of that country. Even in a small country like England, depending on regional differences, people's attitudes differ greatly, and what may be considered good luck in Devon may not be the same as in Leicestershire. Most of our superstition is a mixture of old religious beliefs that have been distorted by Christianity and injected with more sinister meanings. This was their way of trying to brainwash a nation into letting go of the old habits and traditions that were part and parcel of every day life. The saying that a cat has nine lives comes from the number nine being the 'trinity of trinities' – the ultimate in being blessed.

According to *Man, Myth & Magic*, an Italian legend tells of a cat that gave birth to her kittens under the manger in which Jesus was born. "but the cat was not destined to be venerated in Christian Europe, for the Church with its violent repudiation of paganism succeeded in reducing the status of this once sacred animal to that of a devil … During the persecution of the Cathars the belief was fostered that these heretics worshipped the Devil in feline form, and the stage was set for the cat's unwitting participation in the witchcraft tragedy."

More often, cats were given the comparatively minor role of witches' familiars, and the 'wise woman' who took care of the village people as healer and midwife was given the title of witch and hunted down. The domestic cat shared its mistress's punishment and, viewed as having mystical and magical powers, was treated with hatred and could not suffer enough as far as the Church was concerned.

The name 'Grimalkyn' is derived from *grim* or *greom*, a word for the colour grey, and 'Malkin' being a version of the name Maud or Matilda meaning 'cat'. The name was associated with an old female cat that was ill tempered and aggressive in temperament and during the 'Burning Times' women sentenced to death for (heresy) witchcraft were accused of owning a grimalkyn – a name given to a witch's familiar or demon in the form of a cat that had been gifted to her by the devil.

The first written account of the grimalkyn was in William Baldwin's, *Beware of the Cat* (1570) but an older oral association can be found in Scotland where the grimalkyn was thought to be a Faery cat with the same temperament, and has some dark superstition and folklore surrounding it. The tales vary depending on the region but they are thought to stem from the early myths of the ancient Irish-Celtic Tuatha de Dannan, and may explain some of the similarities between the old legends. The brindled cat was also notorious in England as a witch's familiar and in *Macbeth* we find the witches cry: "Thrice the brindled cat hath mewed," while generally speaking the black cat symbolises magic minus malice.

As a result, people in Britain and Europe who were once fond of cats began to look upon them in a different light. Black cats were especially targeted; the belief that a black cat walking across your path will bring bad luck is one of the most common, and in Ireland a black cat walking across your path by moonlight meant a death in an epidemic. In the United States and most of Europe it is regarded as the embodiment of the Devil himself; in many parts of Britain it is the white cat that plays this role. If school-children met a white cat on their way to school they would spit, turn around, and make the sign of the cross to dispel any bad luck that may be brought upon them. In Yorkshire owning a black cat is supposed to be lucky while meeting one by accident on your path is not. If the cat was to walk towards you then it would bring good fortune, but if it walked away then it would take good fortune with it. Even dreaming of a cat was said to bring bad luck. Nevertheless, if a farmer killed a cat then misfortune would befall his cattle, and a cat deserting the household meant there would always be illness. Not everyone thought that black cats were unlucky. Charles I owned a black cat and he was worried that if anything happened to it he would perish so he had the cat guarded day and night. The day after the cat died, he was arrested and later executed.

Another English tradition claims that if a cat sits on the tombstone of someone who has recently died, then their soul was possessed by the devil, but if two cats were seen fighting near a terminally ill person, or on a gravestone, then this meant that the devil and an angel were fighting for the soul of the deceased. If a black cat was seen during a funeral procession then another member of the family would soon die, while in Transylvania if a black cat jumped over a corpse then it would turn into a vampire. In Italy it was believed to be a bad omen if a cat would not stay in the house, because if death was in the air the cat would not want to stick around; if a cat sat on the bed of a sick person then they would die. This was due to the belief that cats could see the spectre of death.

In the Middle Ages, and especially in some areas of France, cats were used as a sacrifice together with other animals on the Summer Solstice bonfires, where a bag or wicker basket of live cats was suspended above a bonfire to be burnt. The embers were then collected and taken home to provide luck and protection for the household. The cat was also associated with the corn spirit and families would tell the children not to go into the field 'as the cat sits there' and when the last sheaves of corn were lifted, it was called 'the cat' or saying 'they had the cat by the tail'. In Dauphine a cat was decked out in ribbons and sheaves of corn at the ceremony of the last cutting and when the feasting was over, the girls of the village would solemnly remove the decorations as a symbol of the end of summer. Sometimes after all the corn was brought in they would kill a cat in the farmyard to ward off evil. The old saying for a woman behaving hysterically 'as having kittens', comes from medieval times when a woman's severe labour pains were believed to be the work of witches, but really she was having kittens.

Due to hysteria and blind superstition the cat has not fared well in Europe and England from the Middle Ages onwards. I have deliberately not gone into the depressing details but it just goes to show the cruelty that these poor creatures have suffered in the name of religion.

But this was not the same worldwide, as the Native Americans believed that dreaming of a cat was a good omen; dreaming of a tortoise-shell cat was thought to be good luck and dreaming of a ginger cat was a sign of wealth and money. Dreaming of tabby cats foretold good fortune in the home. Fishermen's wives would keep a black cat in the house because they believed it would avert any danger to their husbands while at sea. Sailors used to keep cats on the ships as a means of controlling any vermin that might damage the supplies, and an omen states that if the ship's cat approaches the sailor then the voyage will be blessed with good luck - but if the cat only came half way to greet him then bad luck would be in store. The saying that there is 'no space to swing a cat' was born on the seas, and 'the cat' was the small whip with nine 'tails' used to punish seamen - as there was no room to swing the whip inside the ship, the punishment would take place on the deck. We also have weather superstitions from the sailors by observing the cat. If the animal licked its fur against the grain then a hailstorm would happen on the journey; while a sneeze meant rain, and if it was frisky then it forecast winds.

It was not just sailors who would watch the cats for omens.

The ancient Egyptians who thought very highly of the cat and deified it, used to watch for signs of good and bad omens. The Japanese believed the cat to be good luck, especially the Maneki Neko, which was first recorded in the Edo period of Japanese history (1603-1867). These figures are usually made of ceramic and depict a cat on its back legs, waving a paw in the Japanese beckoning fashion. To Westerners it looks like a wave, so those that were imported into the West had the hand turned around. It was known as the beckoning cat, money cat, or lucky cat, and was thought that anyone who owned one was due to gain good luck and money.

These images are placed at the entrance of restaurants and businesses to encourage prosperity, and sometimes show both hands beckoning - the left for gaining customers the right for money and wealth though this may be the opposite depending again on the region. The cats are usually decorated on the ears and bib, some with a scarf or a necklace, but often with a collar and bell. Often they hold a coin called a *koban*, a coin common during the Edo period.

A myth relating how the Siamese cat breed was born was said to come from a temple on Mount Lugj where there lived the Kittah monks who worshipped a golden goddess with sapphire eyes. Her name was Taun- Kyan-Kse. The head monk Mun Ha used to meditate day and night by the statue with his white cat, which had a brown face, paws and tail. At night the monk would go into a deep trance state for reflection but one day invaders killed him when they tried to seize the temple. The cat, which was called Sinh, placed his paw on the monk's robe and his fur turned golden, his eyes a bright sapphire blue; his brown areas turned a lush velvety texture and his paws pure white. The other monks panicked but Sinh spoke up with authority and told them to lock the heavy doors of the temple to prevent any more invaders, and in doing so had saved them all. The next day all the other ninety-nine cats had changed to Sinh's likeness. The cat did not leave his master's side for seven days, when he too died and as a reward attained Nirvana.

The Siamese kings kept the cats of that name sacred and part of the royal family, as it was believed that they would reincarnate as the cat. By contrast, farmers used to carry around the Korat cat, which has silver grey fur like rain clouds, and chant to bring rain to their crops. A poem goes.

The hairs are smooth.
With roots like clouds.
And eyes that shine.
Like dew drops on lotus leaf.

The Magical Cat's Cradle

The game the cat's cradle is probably the oldest game in the world, although its origins are obscure. The aim of the game, which can be played with two people or just with one person, is to make a series of figures by manipulating a piece of string into shapes, and can be kept going until a pattern can be manipulated no longer.

It is played with the first player wrapping the string around one hand or wrist. Then circle it around again. Then take the string that runs down the left arm into the first finger of the right hand. Reach through the triangle that has been created. The first finger of the left hand hooks the right loop. This shape is the cat's cradle.

Player two will then grasp each triangle and pull horizontally with their thumbs and pull them down past the line under the crosses from player one's wrists and back up again. Player one will let go of the string with their finger while player two stretches the string with thumbs and fingers into the shape of the diamond. They can keep on going manipulating different shapes.

The cat's cradle can be a focus for spell casting. Use a piece of string of the desired colour that you wish to use. Focus on the intent and desire while making the movements and creating the patterns until you can make no more. There does not need to be any chanting or words for this. When you have come to the end, remove the completed article from your fingers and place in a safe place until the desired effect is produced. Then either untie or burn the cord. Personally I prefer to do the latter removing every last trace of the spell.

Stepping Into Circle: The Knot Spell

A simpler version of the knot spell is to take a cord of the desired colour and while focusing on the intent tie nine knots in the cord while chanting this universal rhyme.

By this knot of one
The spell has begun.
By this knot of two
It comes true.
By this knot of three
It must be.
By this knot of four
It's empowered more.
By this knot of five
The power thrives.
By this knot of six
This spell I fix.
By this knot of seven
'Tis manna from heaven.
By this knot of eight
It is my fate.
By this knot of nine
My desire is mine.
So mote it be.

Again place the cord in a safe place until the desired effect has been completed. Then either untie the knots or burn the cord.

Herbal Exercise

The magical Tiger Lily has a host of symbolism. The flowers are sometimes yellow or pink, but mostly orange with deep reddish marks and black flecks, which is what gives it its name and association with the tiger - although it has been known to be called Leopard Lily.

Lilies as a whole have a broad spectrum of symbolism but the Tiger Lily represents wealth and prosperity, which links it with the Chinese astrological association of the animal. Some form of wealth attraction can be encouraged in the home by simply having a bunch of the flowers in a vase or growing them in the garden. They are easy to grow, liking either full sun or partial shade in good well-drained soil.

The buds and flowers are edible and when baked taste similar to potatoes. In holistic medicine especially in the East, the Tiger Lily has been used to treat period pains, uterine neuralgia, symptoms of menopause, nausea and vomiting. While also being used as a laxative, they contain anti-bacterial, anti-parasitic and diuretic properties.

From a magical point of view, as well as being used for wealth and prosperity, they are also used for calming aggressive tendencies and balancing. Here is where the pouch can be useful again, by placing Tiger Lily buds inside and carrying it on your person to make use of its properties.

Charm for wealth and prosperity

A simple charm can be made and hung in the hallway near or facing the front door.

- You will need Tiger Lily flowers that have been dried and flattened. This can be done in a heavy unwanted book, because the pollen is very messy, it stains badly and is hard to remove.

- Some thick white card and a glass fronted picture frame.

- Place the flowers flat on the card in a decorative fashion. Place the frame over the card and flowers, seal and hang on a wall facing the front door so it can attract prosperous energy.

Warning: the tiger lily and other lilies' pollen is toxic to cats and can cause vomiting, lethargy, kidney failure and death.

PART FIVE

Feline Sexual Energy

The Cat her familiar spirit, stalks that utter dusk in a form of blackness which is the hue typified by Kali. This is the Night of Time in which are concealed the radiant splendours of the dawning sun ...
[Kenneth Grant, *Aleister Crowley and the Hidden God*]

Sexual energy, while often looked upon with disapproval or distaste, is one of the most natural forms of power that is inherent in all living creatures to maintain the survival of their species. It is also a means of delivering magic for a particular aim as opposed to regular spell casting. This method, however, is either carried out between consenting adults, or by means of masturbation.

The universal symbol of the lion has always been associated with that of lust, and is the strongest and most potent force than in any other species. Aleister Crowley's Tarot, instead of using the card Strength like most tarot decks, made the card Lust for his own deck to encapsulate a much deeper meaning. This is the primitive instinct that is in all human beings and one of the most important and sacred forces which creates life between the opposite sexes. The energy of lust can be felt on many different levels and not just in that of the material world.

The card's meaning conjures up passionate intoxicating, sexual indulgence, losing control of inhibitions, and the setting free from guilt and restraint. The cat, in whatever form, has become the symbol of that lust and fecundity. This is also what Jung meant by the collective unconscious of living things with a similar innate nature. It is not a new concept but has been there since the beginning of man's power to reason. The woman riding the many-headed lion and holding out the grail represents the freedom of her spirit from the shackles of the material world with its moralistic restraints, in order to be enlightened and to progress spiritually.

On a physical level we see how sexual repression has caused a whole host of problems not just in 'open' society but also in controlled environments, such as religious establishments. The result of this repression causes an individual to gain a warped view on sex and disrespect towards other individuals, which in extreme cases can lead to causing not just physical harm, but emotional and psychological harm to others. On a spiritual level, Crowley's Tarot is suggesting we throw off the yoke of 'repressed inherited dogmatic thought' that prevents the soul from moving on to higher things.

For this next exercise we are going to visit the Tarot card Strength again, in order to understand its dual meaning. Previously we visited the card from the point of view of the softer aspects of the goddess Bastet; this time we are going to look at it from another perspective - that of her 'sister' and the more savage aspects of Sekhmet. The aim is to help clarify the dual nature of the solar-lunar feminine force - and how it manifests.

Use the Strength-Lust card and any candle and incense correspondences to aid you in your meditation: the incense is benzoin for Sekhmet and catnip for Bast. Focus your mind on the images on the card and allow yourself to be drawn towards the 'gateway' and see what happens ... ask yourself these questions and keep a record of the results.

- How did you feel?
- Was there anything that stood out for you?
- What 'feeling' did these energies produce?

This Strength-Lust sensation is due to the cat-power no matter what the species. The energies differ in frequency depending on which species is being used for the magical working, but it is always the female of the species that has the strongest and most aggressive elements of the animal's nature.

For example, the female domestic cat (who can be in season several times a year), will advertise this by rolling on the floor and crying out in a fashion designed to attract the male's attention. When males surround her they must approach carefully as she will swipe out at them with her claws. Once a male is close enough he has to grab her at the nape of the neck with his teeth to hold her, and when the mating is over, he must leave quickly otherwise she will attack him.

This is where the goddess Bastet gets her association with fertility, sensuality and promiscuity. Although she is associated with Venus she also has lunar attributes, with cats being thought of as night creatures and hunters. In reality, they actually prefer the half-light of dawn and dusk to hunt – the 'time between times' and the most powerfully charged time of the day for magical working. The lunar association softens the lustful force of the solar cat, but caution must still be taken as the Moon is also the symbol of illusion and false paths.

It appears that the leopard, whether in the form of the spotted variety or that of the black panther, also has an association with the carnal aspects of the human psyche in myth and symbolism. Our example here is in Dante's *Inferno* where on his poetic journey he encounters three creatures: the leopard, who represents fraud with the she-wolf as a symbol of avarice and greed (in some versions the attributes of the she-wolf and leopard are reverse), and the lion who represents lust.

The leopard is represented more by the black panther in myth and symbolism, and the creature's associations also stretch to include the jaguar, and sometimes the cougar. They are a symbol or warning to beware of any weakness in not being able to control desire, natural urges and excesses of the psyche.

The saying that a leopard never changes its spots means that an individual's innate nature cannot change; that an individual will never change even though appearances suggest otherwise. The leopard being a symbol of fraud is to suggest that things are not always what they seem. There are references in the Old Testament suggesting that the silent swiftness of the creature was God's wrath; with the black panther being a symbol of rebirth, trials and tribulations, which is a conflicting image with Dante's analogy.

The force of the panther represents hidden pleasures within us all - a force that was recognised and respected by ancient traditions all over the world. The representation of the panther, as opposed to that of the cat, can be a more aggressive and stronger energy, which can take you into the darkest regions of the psyche. This is where the guidance of a good mentor comes in handy! This energy can also be deceptive and cunning, which can lead an individual to addiction and dependency. We see this in various stories in the media every day of those seeking therapy for issues they feel they are unable to control in themselves.

Dionysus was the god of the vine, his totem animal was said to be that of a panther and he was often depicted wearing a panther skin. Not only the patron of the vine (and wine), he is a symbol of unleashing desires and carnal pleasures; of new awakenings and the knocking down of barriers for freedom with no restraint. Unfortunately, Dionysus also fell into the deceptive trap of overdoing things. At first he drank in moderation, but Hera inflicted upon him a curse of madness in revenge for Zeus's infidelity with Dionysus's mother, he became addicted like a crazed animal.

He overcame his addictive nature by being humbled by a maiden called Amethyst, who refused his advances and had prayed to the gods to help her. It was Artemis who answered her call by turning her into a white stone. Dionysus was so overcome with grief that he poured wine over the stone as an offering and turned the white stone to purple – the amethyst. He went to seek the oracle at Dodona for help with his vices, and on his recovery travelled the world teaching humans the virtues (and, hopefully the downfalls) of wine. The Greeks attributed the amethyst with properties to repel drunkenness in its wearer, and it was later ground down into potions as a tonic for this condition.

It is not just in our physical world that we become subject to slavery in our vices, whether they be chemical or otherwise. It can have a very profound effect on our mental and psychological selves as well. On the physical plane the glamour of these vices can pull us into a world where nothing else matters but the need to gratify this addiction. Whatever the vice, it can lead to an individual becoming isolated and depressed with morbid or deranged thoughts.

Likewise going on a spiritual or magical journey there are points where the student comes across the dark Void of despair from which they feel unable to escape. It is all too easy and tempting to give up. Panther-power can teach us to be strong, to fight through the darkness and to understand the illusions that are contained within the Void. This is *usual* on a spiritual or magical quest, and understanding of what has happened doesn't come about until the student gets that flash of inspiration to show that they have come out the other side. The black panther is both sides of the coin. It will show you the vices and the dark spots of the hidden persona while guiding you towards that flash of inspiration that will change your life. How you deal with it is up to you.

The power of sexual femininity and the deepest secrets of the female body were held sacred by many ancient cultures. In India and Babylonia, and indeed in some Hindu sects today, there were temples where the Tantric priests and priestesses understood and practiced the sacred and magical connections of sexual energy in both its physical and spiritual form. It is said that the priestesses would prostitute themselves in order to utilize these energies so that they were able to gain deeper spiritual insights. Here is where the definition of the word 'whore' came from - and before anyone starts throwing their hands up in disgust, the word originally meant 'beloved' or 'beloved one'.

The woman whom we equate with Crowley's Scarlet Woman, Babylon's name actually means 'the gate'. Her secret gate is the vagina, which holds the mysteries that she willingly allows the solar male energy-force to enter through - the 'gate', 'cut', or 'cat'. The cat as we are aware is the symbol of the Moon and a reflection of the Sun's energies.

There were also specific priestesses who would take part in the ritual at different phases of the moon, as magical energy is different depending on each day the moon passes through its cycle. This art, and the priests and priestesses who were involved in its practice, treated it as a very sacred magical act. In fact, many of the rituals happened when there was no actual physical contact between the sexes at all. It was about controlling the mind and this energy is known as *kundalini*.

Neither should the 'Dark of the Moon' be dismissed or ignored, as sometimes happens in today's modern magic. This region holds the deepest hidden meanings of passion, which can, if not controlled and used properly cause an overspill of unbridled base desires within us all. This is the birthplace of the *kundalini*, the fire snake that is ignited within the chakra at the base of the spine – where it is coiled around three times waiting to be opened. The Hindus believe that the goddess Kundalini-Shakti governs this chakra, called the *shushuma*, which is at the very root of the spine in the prostate or lower ovarian area. She represents the unfolding of the 'Shakti' energy that enlivens potential life. Although the form usually takes that of the great fire serpent rising through the body, sometimes she is seen in the form of the black panther - the power-animal of the dark mother goddess form.

WARNING: To invoke this energy with no guidance or

tutorship can cause problems. An out of control *kundalini* can cause not just manifestations in sexual deviance but left open the overpowering *kundalini* can result in depression and self destruction. You have been warned.

Anyone who wishes to follow a serious study in Tantra would be wise to find a reputable tutor. But be careful as there are a lot of charlatans out there – so the school and/or tutor must come on a recommendation. There is the temptation in this day and age for students to try and gain all of their knowledge from books or the internet. While the web holds a whole host of information about the subject some can be conflicting and sometimes confusing for a would-be student. This is a true magical art and like any other magical path there has to be safe working guidelines that only a genuine tutor can give. Also the Inner Mysteries will *never* be put up on a website - they have to be earned just like everything else. Like the old saying goes: if a student is ready the tutor will come.

Many ancient cultures including the Egyptians used sex magic in their rites in varying forms and not just for fertility. They also knew just how potent a rite enacted by the orgasmic climax really could be. A lot of training was involved in this area, as when using magic in this form, great control is needed to direct the power of the magic to its target without getting lost in the throes of the moment. Doing this could lead to the energy dispersing in all areas except where you want it to go!

The Egyptians did have a means of being able to tell the time by the menstrual cycle and it did not take them long to link this to the lunar cycle. As Kenneth Grant puts it "Time is the *menstruum* to which all material forms arise, transform and finally dissolve. The menstrual blood is highly magical and is said to be used in spells for transmutation to bring on change magically." It was also believed to be used in darker magic and was an essential ingredient in the rites of the Hindu goddess, Kali - another aspect of the dark goddess of death and destruction.

Stepping Into Circle: The Summoning of Ose

Ose is the fifty-seventh spirit of the *Goetia* and one of three whose form comes in the appearance of a leopard. Ose is a great president and commands 31 legions of spirits. He first appears as a leopard though at the command of the magician will take the appearance of a man. He has the ability to make "one cunning in the liberal arts and sciences", while also to be able to change the form of an individual. In the chapter where I have described a method of taking on animal form, this symbol could be taken into the circle as a point of focus.

He is able to transform an individual so that they will take on the *nature* of the animal without even realising this. It may be best when employing Ose for such workings to have another individual present to keep an eye on proceedings. When summoned, Ose can give true answers to divine questions but don't ask the question if you are unprepared for the truth. Ose can be very cunning and deceptive if not commanded firmly. Bear this in mind when using this spirit and make sure you close down properly when the session is over.

Herbal Exercise

A natural cat 'high' that can easily be grown in the garden is catnip or cat mint. (*nepira catira*). We don't know why this particular plant makes cats react the way they do. Rolling around the floor and even chasing and biting their own tails. But it sends them on a 10 minute high where some really strange and funny behaviour is seen. After which they come down back to normal like nothing has happened.

Catnip can be used medicinally as well as magically.

Medicinally it can be taken as a tea to promote calmness as it has mild sedative properties. It was thought in ancient times to be a good cure for colic though this has not been clinically proven. It can be taken to help with adult digestion issues; sew the leaves into little pillows and place them under your own pillow to help promote sleep.

Magically catnip is a herb associated with Bastet, water, the planet Venus, love, beauty and mild intoxication. If attempting to utilise cat-power catnip can be burned in incense form and combined with mugwort for a stronger effect. Having the plant in the home or garden can be an aid to attract beauty and calming energies to the home.

Catnip can be used in love spells, but can also be used for more than that - used in a mojo bag with dragon's blood powder to break an addiction or obsession, especially that of a love interest that is ill matched, has no hope of going anywhere, or is disastrous to a person. To promote self love and find your own inner beauty, which in turn will lead to self confidence and self worth, make up a mojo bag of catnip and carry this around with you.

PART SIX

Celestial Associations and Magical Correspondences

The cat went here and there
and the moon spun round like a top,
and the nearest kin of the moon,
the creeping cat, looked up.
Black Minnaloushe stared at the moon,
for, wander and wail as he would,
the pure cold light in the sky
troubled his animal blood.
The Cat and the Moon, W B Yeats

In the Western zodiac the lion is represented by the sign Leo, with the associating and ruling planet being the Sun. The Sun is the centre of our solar system and everything revolves around it. It provides heat, warmth and life to the earth and is an awesome presence that eclipses the heavens when it shines by day.

Lions in Western Astrology

In a general sense those who are born under this sign are immensely popular. If they are not, then they think there is something wrong as they crave respect and attention. Leos are at their best when in a position of authority/responsibility where they can shine and those under them will quite happily follow their lead. However, if things are not going their way they can lose interest and actively loath what they are doing – but they will soon get over it and move onto the next big project as Leos are very practical and spiritual, and see things from different perspectives that help them in their life and work.

Female Leos tend to wear the trousers in a relationship. They have to be at the centre and in control of their world whether it is work or home. They also like their independence, and money to them is only important as a means of realizing their goals and dreams and not the be all and end all of everything.

Magical correspondences for the energies of Leo are: Ruling planet the sun; metal is gold and gemstone is amber. In numerological terms the Sun and all its aspects are ruled by the number 1. Its vibrations are also linked to that of leadership, authority and great ambition. The number 1 has great strength, is motivated, bold and persuasive. In the word 'lion' and 'Leo' the letters add up to five. This is where the unpredictable fun-loving aspects of the personality is shown. Number 5 also has the potential to enjoy pleasure especially that of lust and sex, which is characteristic with the traits of Leo; which in turn is linked with the traits of the lion and its natural behaviour. As we can see everything is universally linked in one way or another.

Generally speaking, with Leo being a fire sign, Air signs like Aquarius, Gemini and Libra are the most compatible, with Aquarius being the most favourable.

While there are positive connections in most signs with each other, some are more compatible than others. Leo-Libra is a good combination in that they both enjoy a warm loving relationship, however Leo is the more dominant of the two and so the stronger partner. While Libra is more flexible, they will protest if Leos go too far!

Leo-Gemini are really good friends and compatible lovers, with both having a fun side that works in harmony. Leos love to be the centre of their partner's or friend's universe, this can cause problems as Geminis need a wide range of friends and interests to keep them going. There is also the problem of a Leo needing to be taken seriously ... which for Gemini can be difficult.

Leo-Aquarius is the best match of them all although on paper it does not look very likely. The Leo loves the Aquarian intellectual mind and the fact that they are very different. Although cool and aloof, the Aquarian while thinking that Leos are self - centred and take themselves too seriously, loves their energy and lust for life. With the Leo liking everything to evolve around *them* and considering personal relationships to be personal, will dislike the Aquarian need for a large network of friends, and the Aquarian doing exactly what they want to do. Unlike Leo, the Aquarian has a very laid back attitude but the combination works because between them, they bring everything into a relationship and can learn from each other.

Leo and the other two fire signs Aries, and Sagittarius are passionate on a sexual level but can also be very destructive in a relationship. The other two can be harsh and not spare the feelings of the over sensitive Leo. Water signs are not ideal either, as they don't draw attention to themselves, and would dislike the constant attention-seeking attitudes of the Leo. Leo and Earth signs don't really fair much better as earth signs are immovable and stubborn. They are very down to earth and practical, and will soon put the Leo in his/her place.

Tigers in Chinese Astrology

In Chinese mythology the zodiac works on a cycle of twelve animals each having a rulership over a one year period. It was said that Buddha called all the animals to him so he could honour them. Only 12 showed up. To thank them he gave them a year where anyone born within this year would have the psychological characteristics of the animal whose year it was. The year would be named after this animal and the vibrations that the year heralded would equate to the animal's behaviour

The animals argued as to who was going to be first and which order they would go in during the representation of the cycle. So Buddha told them that they should have a race to cross the river and the first one across would be the first to have a year named after them ... so the race began, the tiger being the third animal to reach the far shore.

In China the tiger is the king of the animals much like a lion is in the African and western countries. His fur and stripes represent the Yin and Yang lines that are prevalent in the Chinese *I Ching* philosophy (*The Book of Changes*). He is the protector of children and drives away demons. He is a mark of strength with a white tiger being a symbol of royal valour. As the tiger is a symbol of greatness, it can also be a symbol of terror and destruction - of hidden dangers waiting to strike.

Those born in that year have traits of loyalty courage and generosity: they like to be the boss of anything in work, home, and friends. They have to learn self-control and moderation as they are the type of people who like to take risks. The Wisdom says that those born under this sign at night will be calmer and much wiser than those who are born during the day - who will be more unpredictable. They are honourable but do not like a mundane life, although they will cope with it due to the fact that they hate failure. Tigers are very generous as long as those they associate with are honourable as they do not like falsehood and lies, those who are traitors to their values will be cut off and disowned. This type of person would be wise to stay well clear of those born under the year of the Tiger as they are likely to be brought down with a very strong paw.

Magical correspondences for the energies of the Tiger are the eastern version of the Lion in most of its aspects and energy. The correspondences are those of the solar energy of strength, pride and bravery. The colour is orange, although tiger's eye is a stone associated with the tiger more for its multi-banded colouring. The number 5 is its numerical value; and benzoin its incense. If we are using this power animal's energies in conjunction along with the I Ching, we would have to consider its relationship with the five sacred elements of the system: fire, metal, wood, earth and air.

Gemstone: Tiger's Eye

Tiger's eye is a stone for protection and was traditionally carried as a talisman for protection against ill wishes and curses. It is yellow and black striped, which gives it its name, and reflects the creature's eye. With the tiger being a protector of territories this is an ideal stone to be carried with you in a little string bag in your purse, or as a small piece of jewellery. It is also the birth-stone for the zodiac sign Gemini, which reflects the dual nature of the tiger.

The Jaguar in Mayan and Aztec Astronomy

The jaguar is one of the most important creatures in the daily and spiritual lives of the Maya and Aztec, and here we have a fine example of a power animal used in a tradition where shamanism was part of the people's day-to-day lives. The jaguar's spots were said to represent the stars of the Milky Way which was associated with the sky- mother, and the 'mouth of the cat' was the dark spot within the Milky Way, which is in fact a 'black hole' located near Sagittarius - the galactic centre of the Milky Way, which the Central Americans believed was the source of all life.

The Mayans were a literate people whose empire stretched across Central America from around 2000 BC to 250 AD and from archaeological discoveries on wall paintings, statues and pottery there is evidence of worship of jaguars in varying forms. In certain areas of Mayan culture they represented the Sun as it rose in the east and prowled the day growing older as the day wore on. Old and tired in the west it would set, only to have to fight Xibalba, who was the god of the Underworld. Victorious the Sun would rise again in the east to give light to the world.

The Mayans had a dual meaning for the jaguar in that their coats represented the starry heavens and the jaguar-spirit prowled the night sky. A demonstration of the jaguar's ability to cross over into different worlds: the living and the earth belonged to the day world, while the spirit and ancestors were of the night world. A jaguar deity that represented each of these realms was regarded as necessary in the Cycle of Life. Both were regarded as helpers of the Creator to establish what was needed in the continuing cycle of the world.

The God 'L' who was reputed to be the god of terrestrial fire was also an Underworld deity and had the eyes of a jaguar with a *cruller*, (a doughnut shaped loop), around the nose ears and fangs. He was thought to preside over black magic and is possibly one of the oldest of the Mayan deities. A demi-god associated with childbirth, whose symbol was the ears and tail of a jaguar and sometimes represented with a *cruller*, is the suggested spouse of 'L'. She was also identified as a moon goddess at some point during Mayan history, being responsible for the rains to help crops to grow and feed the people; while in her association with the moon she was sometimes given another name; for her this was the Rainbow Lady. In contrast, there was a protector god in the form of a giant jaguar with a water lily on his head, who was the protector of the king.

For the shaman, the jaguar was a representation of strength and protection. They were *naguals*, which means 'spirit guides', to act as guide through the realms of Otherworld, and jaguar skins were worn by priest and kings for this very reason. It enabled the shaman to take on the attributes of the jaguar while he went into his trance state. Shamans were also big believers in shape shifting into the form of the cat and roaming the forests, skies and heavens while also being able to travel through the other realms and dimensions unhindered.

To the Aztecs, Tzcallipoca, who was a major deity of these people was a god who had many facets to his power. His sacred animal was the jaguar and when he was in this form he was known as Tepeyollotl, which meant 'mountain heart'. His name is translated to 'smoking mirror', which is a link to the stone obsidian that was (and still are) used as scrying mirrors. Tzcallipoca was depicted as having a yellow and black striped face with one foot depicted either as a snake or a mirror, with the mirror sometimes in the place of his heart. This image was used as a symbol of him fighting the earth monster. Representative of the northern direction of the night winds, hurricanes, war, temptation, strife and night sky, he was also a patron of rulership, the earth and divination.

Magical correspondences for the energies of the Jaguar are a little different from any other cat. When viewing it as a solar energy moving across the sky like the sun, the Element is Fire - the life-giving fertility force with orange as its colour. When viewing its stellar aspect, the fire is the fire of creativity, with the colours of midnight blue and gold. The jaguar is also the night hunter and deity of the dark realms of death and Otherworld, associated with the colour black and Element of Earth. The energy can also be identified with storms and destruction and therefore with the Element of Water and the colour of blue-grey. Its speed and agility gives it the Element of Air with the colour of yellow.

Placing a numerical value on the jaguar is not as straight forward ...to the ancient peoples its energy was both male *and* female ... it was associated with all the elements ... it lived in this world and the next and was responsible for life, death and rebirth. The most appropriate number that can be assigned to it is that of zero - the cosmic number of the universe, as that from where life comes from and where it returns. Being feline the incenses are benzion in its harsher form; or catnip in its softer.

The Celestial Cats

There are four representations of felines in the heavens: the constellations of Felis, Leo (major and minor) and the Lynx.

The Lynx

The *Accademia dei Linca*, or Academy of Lynxes, or the Lincian

Academy of science founded in 1603 in Rome is one of the oldest dwellings of scientific learning in the world and its emblem is that of the Lynx, whose sharp vision was essential in the study of science. In medieval times it was believed that the lynx's urine would dry out and crystallize into a gemstone. We can, therefore say that the symbolism of the lynx is not just that of strength and stealth but also that of a quest for knowledge that we wish to undertake. This is the knowledge on all levels of life whether scientific or esoteric, or of things that have been forgotten or hidden; even the ability to walk through these hidden realms to find self-discovery.

The Lynx, however, is a modern constellation, created in the late seventeenth century by the astronomer, Hevelius, who claimed that you had to be lynx-eyed to see it, as it contains no bright stars, even though it covers a large area. Therefore, to see a lynx as an omen could be a warning to be on guard against an individual, or to look deeper at a certain situation or person since things may not always be as they seem.

If journeying on a path working or meditation, listen and follow the lynx as it will lead you to what you wish to know whether this information be in a symbolic form or a direct answer. The Lynx is found in the northern sky; and faintly hidden, it can be found between Ursa Major and Auriga.

The Cat

Felis – the Cat – is no longer included in modern star charts, but was created by the astronomer Jerome Lalande who, having been perplexed by the stars throughout his life, and being very fond of cats, announced that he would now have his joke and let the Cat scratch the 'starry chart' (*The Box of Stars*, Catherine Tennant). The Cat was situated towards the head of Hydra, the Water Serpent, and Antlia, and was included in the c1825 publication of *Urania's Mirror*. There are no known magical associations or correspondences.

Leo Major

The constellation of Leo is viewed in the southern sky in spring and is very close to the equator with Canis Major to the north-west above it. Regulus, the brightest star was thought to be lucky in ancient European and Asian countries; it seems to have gained the title 'ruler of the heavens' that denotes power, riches and glory and was also known as 'the king's star'. Indeed in many ancient cultures the constellation was associated with the lion - the Babylonians calling it *ur gula*, the great lion and the Persians who knew it as *ser* or *shir* which also means 'lion'.

In Egypt the rising of the constellation coincided with the annual floods, possibly because at this time lions moved in from the deserts to drink. As lions were considered a representation of the great Father Gods and the goddess Sekhmet, and symbolised life-giving properties, it was considered a blessing and a great omen to see the lion at the waterside. This also suggests why statues and temples were built at locations by the riverside and at water holes in desert areas. They even erected fountains with water coming from the lion's mouth in keeping with the symbolism – which is still fashionable today.

The tail star, Denabola, in contrast was thought to bring tidings of bad omens and was very unlucky. This star can be found in the tail of the lion constellation while Regulus is located in the heart area.

Leo Minor

The Little Lion is a new invention, created in the seventeenth century. It has no real myths attached to it, although this part of the sky was thought by the ancient Egyptians, to be sacred to the great god Ptah. There are no known magical associations or correspondences.

Stepping Into Circle: Scrying

Scrying is a very ancient art that gives glimpses into Otherworld.

It not only gives visual/symbolic answers to our questions, but can also put us into contact with Otherworld beings to aid us on our spiritual path. To some it may be easy. To others it requires a lot of practice. There are many different ways to scry. One simple and cheap way is using a bowl with a black interior filled with water. You can either light a candle and focus on the reflection in the water, or if the moon is out and especially when it is full, take the bowl outside and focus on the reflection cast by the moonlight.

Sit for a while and focus on the bowl and see if any images appear – either in the bowl or in your mind in the form of a suggestion. When you have finished your meditation, always make sure you close the door to that realm to prevent anything from coming through into our world that really shouldn't be here! Whatever form you use, cross your hands in front of you palms down, and move them outwards as if to clear away the energy or close the door. One simple scrying method I discovered accidentally was when I went to the swimming baths and sat on the edge looking into the ripples of the pool. They became very hypnotic and I could have stayed there all afternoon if it wasn't for my friends harassing me to get in.

The traditional form is to use a crystal ball, which, surprisingly is not always of the clear quartz crystal variety. Dr John Dee and Edward Kelly when using this method to contact the 'beings' who gave them the Enochian Keys, used smoky quartz and this is often thought to be one of the best crystals to work with for this purpose. However I have an obsidian ball acquired a few years ago that does the trick for me: I light a candle and just as with a bowl of water, focus on the reflection.

The mirror used for scrying is one that has a black face. It does not have to be of obsidian but it can be a mirror that is painted black. Mirrors, however, are for those who have had considerable practice at using scrying tools, since they can be harmful for those who can easily 'see' but who don't have the required experience of moving into and out of these realms. Without sounding melodramatic, 'something' could very easily be brought back from this plane that could potentially harm an individual physically as well as mentally. It is possible also for individuals to be lost in these outer planes and never able to find their way back. The result is that the 'shell' left behind does not respond physically or mentally to anything around it, and the next stop could be an institution.

It is always wise to keep a record of what you have seen in your journal, because although it may not appear to be important at that moment, at some point in the future another experience may connect with what you had seen in the mirror. Do not loose heart if you cannot get anything to come through at first, it *does* take practice and sometimes trying too hard can be a cause in itself. It is also wise to keep the balls and mirrors that are used for scrying purposes covered up with a black cloth, or wrapped up in a silk cloth and placed in a draw out of reach of inquiring hands.

Herbal Exercise

Cat's tail, of which there are many varieties of species is widely found around rivers and lakes throughout North America. It has long blade shaped leaves with long brown cigar shaped flowers up to a foot long. Most of the plant is edible and has provided a major food source for the Native American people, containing a rich source of vitamins and minerals essential for health. It is believed to have anti-inflammatory properties and aids stomach problems such as neutralizing stomach lactose and aids the healing of stomach ulcers. Externally it is thought to heal bruises, sores and wounds pretty rapidly.

Magically, cat's tail is associated with the Element of Fire; the colour is red, and the primal energy is lust. This force is encountered during sex magic and can be directed by using the power of the *kundalini* - the coiled fire-serpent that exists within all of us. This technique is used in eastern Tantric traditions and is not just used as an aid in sex magic but also as a tool for personal spiritual growth.

Conclusion: The Cat as a Power-Animal

As Mélusine Draco acknowledges in *Black Horse, White Horse* and *Aubry's Dog* in shamanic terms, everyone is believed to have power animals – guardians that empathize with us, guide us on the spiritual path, and protect us from harm. Each power animal increases our inner power by giving access to the wisdom of its kind, so that negative energy cannot influence our thoughts and actions. A horse guardian will impart 'horse sense', and endow us with some of the attributes of a horse; a dog guardian will give 'dog sense', and bestow some of the instincts of a dog.

We have to remember whilst looking at cats from a magical point of view that these power animals also have their own energies and the forces they generate are *very* powerful. This power is aligned to their individual behaviour patterns and has been imprinted in their DNA from the dawn of their existence. The subtle differences in the power between the species are also due to the habitat in which they have learned to operate. A leopard-power may be suited to a particular working where jaguar-power may not. At first glance they may seem very similar, and do share some physical and behavioural features, but their magical energies are very different indeed. This is also evident for anyone wanting to find a feline power-animal, as it is usually the case that the power-cat in question finds the seeker and not the other way around.

Jaguar path working

The jaguar, as we have seen, was the ancient mother-goddess of the Indian tribes of South America, who saw her body as that of the Milky Way. This path working is designed to align ourselves with the oldest energy of the universe. The native Americans were not the only people to identify the stars as being the source of magical power and the birthplace of everything. The ancient

Egyptian goddess Nut was also a stellar-mother.

Find a nice clear night, the best being during the autumn and winter in the northern hemisphere, when there is no moon and more of the stars are visible. We can either sit or lie outside preferably on something comfortable and be wrapped up warm as the cold can put us off our working.

Pick out a bright star in any constellation as it was believed that all the stars in the Milky Way were the body of the jaguar due to the rosettes on its body. We focus deeply on this star and have the jaguar in mind while we move deeper and deeper into the star. Everything around us starts to melt away as we move closer and closer to it. As we focus we become aware of the movement in the shape of the jaguar traced out within the pattern of the stars. We follow and see where it will lead. In this path working we need to keep an open mind. Time as we know it on Earth does not exist in Space. There is also a chance of inter-galactic astral travel that is not the same as in the usual sense of a path working. When you have finished your journeying move out of the void by slowly bringing that one star into view and moving outwards and back into the present day. You could have been sat there for minutes or hours as is the case with these workings. Have a hot drink and a biscuit to ground yourself and warm up before returning to the normal mundane. This should be done after any magical exercise to ensure you are back in the physical realm and not stuck somewhere in between.

Record any experiences you have in a journal. Do not worry if you don't get anything first time. It takes a bit of practice for some. The experience and feelings from any path workings are personal and one experience will differ from another, as we are all individuals. Working with the jaguar is very unique in that the forces of this power animal connects us with the universal force of creativity. Anyone who has any interest in Crowley's Thelemic tradition may appreciate the similarities in the vibration of these forces and may wish to adopt the jaguar as a power animal to aid their journey into magical discovery.

Different Points of Contact

Some individuals may still be looking for their animal guide. The best way to do this is with the section on discovering totem animals that I have explained earlier in the book. However some may prefer to practice visualisation in a path working, in which we go into the environment of a particular cat and get a feel for them this way. It can also help if we wish to gain messages from them. Most of the feline species are solitary, unless you prefer to work with the lion which lives in a pride; the practitioner would have their work cut out as instead of having one animal as a subject of focus she/he would have the whole family in the path-working, as these animals never do anything on their own! That is unless you find a nomad: a young solitary male lion which has just left its mother and is looking for a pride of his own.

Here is a path working with a tiger.

Tigers are solitary and use vast areas of territory to wander in, where they prefer to remain hidden, relying on stealth to hunt their prey. With their ability for stealth it makes an interesting journey to discover *this* power-animal.

We need to find a time where we will not be disturbed. We take long deep breaths as our body consciously begins to sink deep down ... and relaxes; breathing out clearing away all the aspects of the physical world. We then imagine ourselves standing in front of a large canvass – an oil painting of a tropical rain forest. There are huge green trees, tall leafy plants and vines, and vivid colours all shaded as the sunlight is blocked out by the tall and ancient trees.

Walking slowly towards the canvas we step over the frame, are now transported into the heart of the forest, and what immediately hits us is the heat. We are aware of a fine mist of moisture from the regular rains that keep the forest so lush. We are also conscious of the sounds of the forest: a chatter of tropical birds and small monkeys in the trees - we cannot see them but we can see branches of the trees moving. Have a walk around for a while - being careful not to fall over tree roots, get tangled in vines and all the time watching out for dips in the ground. With the vegetation being so thick it is hard to see where to walk.

We keep going forward until we come to a small opening fringed with long tall grasses. The area is much brighter but the sky is misty from the rains. Then we hear a rumble of a roar in the distance. While we try to gage the distance of the roar, walk carefully as we spot a river to our right. We walk slowly towards the water, ever mindful of the dangers as this is also crocodile country. Suddenly we become aware of eyes watching and something moving towards us where we stand. At first it was ahead to the left but is moving further round to the left and coming straight at us.

We have nowhere to go for a place of safety; the river is behind us with trees to the left and long grass to the right. The grass sways and as we look forward a slight movement is detectable. Then a huge pair of yellow eyes. We have met the king of the Eastern jungle. The tiger is a creature of pride, strength and royalty but there is a hidden side to the animal-power behind those stripes that cannot be fathomed unless an individual is brave enough to get close. Neither is it possible to gage his mood, although he can empower us with great wisdom and strength if we are brave enough. Whatever happens next is up to us ... When you are ready to leave, turn around to break the contact; find the picture frame and step out.

- **Make sure you record the results of these journeys in your journal. Some of the answers you seek may not be immediately apparent but may become clear after some time.**

These are just two examples of how different feline energies can be, and the same consideration should be taken when working spells or rituals. We have to be sure the energy we are using is right for the job! Using the wrong energy can cause disastrous results in the outcome of a working or it may not work at all.

Spell to find a speedy solution and a direct route to a goal

This spell is aided by the energy of the cheetah, and is for when you are stuck in finding solutions to situations. This will help you to find the focus for the goal. It can also be useful in situations where you need a fast and direct approach to a particular goal when you are faced with obstacles that are slowing down your progress i.e. a house move where solicitors are dragging their feet and you need to move by a particular date. Remember that the speed and focus that comes with the cheetah's energy only works in short bursts and is not to be used for anything that requires longevity. You will need:

A yellow candle.
Pen and paper.
Palm oil.
Marjoram incense.

Take the yellow candle and anoint it with the palm oil. While anointing it think of your intended goal and visualize it happening. Light the candle and incense. Write on the piece of paper the goal and the outcome you wish to achieve. Hold the paper over the flame while still visualizing and say:

Run through darkness, run through light.
Run until my goal's in sight.
Let no hurdles bar my way.
Faster, faster, clear my way.

So mote it be.

While still focusing place the paper into the flame of the candle and as it burns imagine the smoke forming the body of the cheetah taking your spell and running with it. Let the candle burn itself out. Make sure you are fully committed to the outcome you seek as once this spell is in motion it cannot be returned.

I hope I have revealed the magical nature and powers of the cat family. How they became part of the world of humans, and how they have imprinted themselves on our unconscious minds - whether they are a part of a magical or mystical tradition, or just as loved members of our family. The cat is here to stay whether people love them or hate them. They have a lot to teach us especially those who embrace them as power animals and learn to respect them on the deeper levels of the mind.

In tribal cultures, in which both the shaman and the witch have their distant roots, the power animal is an individual's 'other self', a creature to which that person's life is inextricably bound by common ancestry. And it is therefore important to honour our 'power cat' as such. Unfortunately, in modern cultures we are not taught to value animals, or to acknowledge the gifts that they bring into our lives – and the world around us. On a personal level, by honouring our 'power cat' we acknowledge that otherworldly binding; that the spirit of the animal is giving up its 'freedom' in order to enhance our spiritual development. This can be as simple as saying a silent 'thank you'; or acquiring an object that represents our 'power cat' and putting it where we can interact with it as we go about our daily tasks. By honouring our 'power cat' we make a deeper connection with it on both spiritual and temporal levels that will last a lifetime ... and those lifetimes to come.

About the Author

Martha Gray has studied the magical arts under the direction of Mélusine Draco, and is now a senior tutor within the Coven of the Scales – a magical group inaugurated by Bob and Mériém Clay-Egerton in the 1980s. She lives with her family – feline and human – in Derbyshire. www.covenofthescales.com

Moon Books invites you to begin or deepen your encounter with Paganism, in all its rich, creative, flourishing forms.